# Self Discovery

## The Most Powerful Collection of Self Discovery

*(A Step-by-step Guide to Help People Find Themselves)*

**Sherryl Francis**

Published By **Bengion Cosalas**

## Sherryl Francis

All Rights Reserved

*Self Discovery: The Most Powerful Collection of Self Discovery (A Step-by-step Guide to Help People Find Themselves)*

## ISBN 978-1-77485-557-7

No part of this guidebook shall be reproduced in any form without permission in writing from the publisher except in the case of brief quotations embodied in critical articles or reviews.

Legal & Disclaimer

The information contained in this ebook is not designed to replace or take the place of any form of medicine or professional medical advice. The information in this ebook has been provided for educational & entertainment purposes only.

The information contained in this book has been compiled from sources deemed reliable, and it is accurate to the best of the Author's knowledge; however, the Author cannot guarantee its accuracy and validity and cannot be held liable for any errors or omissions. Changes are periodically made to this book. You must consult your doctor or get professional medical advice before using any of the suggested remedies, techniques, or information in this book.

Upon using the information contained in this book, you agree to hold harmless the Author from and against any damages, costs, and expenses, including any legal fees potentially resulting from the application of any of the information provided by this guide. This disclaimer applies to any damages or injury caused by the use and application, whether directly or indirectly, of any advice or information presented, whether for breach of contract, tort, negligence, personal injury, criminal intent, or under any other cause of action.

You agree to accept all risks of using the information presented inside this book. You need to consult a professional medical practitioner in order to ensure you are both able and healthy enough to participate in this program.

**Table of contents**

Introduction .................................1

Chapter 1: Utilizing Journals For Self-Discovery .............................5

Chapter 2: Importance Of Handwriting In Your Journal ..........18

Chapter 3: Starting To Journal ........28

Chapter 4: Recording Your Goals....41

Chapter 5: Do Not Give Up And Keep Focused On The Goal......................59

Chapter 6: Arduous Yet Nevertheless Worthy Path To Take ......................64

Chapter 7: Writing To Control Emotions .........................................70

Chapter 8: Writing To Determine Emotional Triggers..........................84

Chapter 9: The Journaling Technique To Discover Self-Development .....100

Chapter 10: Declarate Yourself Connect To Your Vision And Trust The Process ...................................115

Chapter 11: An Unexpected Companion - When Conscience Meet Tranquillity ...................................147

Chapter 12: Determine Your Purpose - Define Your "Why" .....................165

Conclusion ...................................182

### Introduction

Are you looking forward to your life being be transformed. You're sure you want to experience something that works differently however, you're not sure what to do. There is a desire to alter the way you move through life however, figuring out how to accomplish this is a major hassle without an initial point of reference. If you're having trouble with your own life, have you considered what you're about? There's a reason why numerous contemplative people have taken time to think "Who is you?" on more than one occasion. A lot of times, we become distracted in our everyday lives. We lose sight of being aware of the person we truly are and in the process we lose our authentic selves. We lose sight of our values, hopes and goals.

It's not fair to anyone, and definitely isn't something you can ignore. If you're hoping to attain satisfaction, you must understand who you are on a personal level. You must discover the person you lost and you must determine the best way to bring yourself back to that place and ensure that you're able to be in touch with your most intimate thoughts. There are ways to do this and will not take you long and interminable hours. You can actually accomplish this in 10-15 minutes per day, if you want to. If you're only able to spare just five minutes, it's sufficient to connect with yourself once more. But the catch is that you must do it.

regularly.

Journaling is a topic that's in the spotlight and, in this book you'll be able to discover the reasons to take the time to journal and the ways to ensure that you adhere to your journaling routine. Journaling is among the most effective practices you can develop to keep connected to your self. It allows you express your emotions as you begin to know yourself better, and much more. It will help you get rid of the clutter you are thinking about to keep yourself from getting overwhelmed and there's a beautiful simplicity in journaling. If you're looking to begin journaling the best thing to do is to get comfortable with the habit of journaling and let the pen fly over your paper. It's not that difficult, and definitely isn't difficult in any way. All you have to do is willing to give it a go and you'll find that there's a beneficial outcome!

In this book, we'll examine a variety of important aspects to think about when you do this. We will also discuss ways to make use of journals to discover yourself, and why it is strongly recommended to write with your hands in your journals, rather than some other form. We will cover the steps to journal and also how you can create a routine you can follow to stay in the right direction. We will then begin to dive into. The book we're taking a look at six different areas to consider tackling. They include writing down your goals to conquer challenges, monitor progress, manage your emotions, to pinpoint your emotional triggers and to begin to discover yourself. In each chapter, you will find details about each subject and ways you can start to tackle these issues, along with numerous journaling prompts that can be used to trust in case you aren't sure the right way to go about it or aren't sure the best way to start. Journaling is a safe process and you'll quickly see that it's worthwhile if you decide to try it!

If you study the book, you'll realize that journaling can be significantly better than what you imagined! Journaling can be a great way to learn about yourself , and to make sure that you're improving yourself and becoming more successful in your personal projects.

Thank you for reading this book. I'm hoping you will be able to achieve your goals and see the most effective results from you.

## Chapter 1: Utilizing Journals For Self-Discovery

So. You're trying to understand yourself. Maybe, you're doing it because someone has said it would assist you in your efforts to "chill down" or "feel more positive" concerning something. In reality, it is a great way to do this when you're ready to move ahead. However, you might be thinking you to yourself: how do you begin to know yourself better through writing? Do you not already have the thoughts you write down in your journal, without needing to record them?

Well, sure. However, you might discover that you've forgotten many of the things you had in mind. It is possible that your thoughts do not seem to be coherent when there's no tidy pattern laid out for you to see. In reality, when you write your thoughts on paper, you'll have an actual record of your thoughts. You can revisit them. You can revisit them whenever you're feeling down. It is possible to go through what you're feeling currently to help you know how you came to that point and why you're there and what you can do to change it. Understanding the thoughts you were using prior to this is an excellent way to start learning about yourself, your thoughts, how you process your thoughts, and much more.

In this chapter, we're going to look at journaling as a process. We'll take time to explore different forms of journaling, and why it is so important. We will also discuss the process of self-reflection that happens in journaling and how crucial that process is when it comes to understanding you, the things that are in your head and the best way to reconnect with your self again. The more you work through this process, the simpler it gets and you shouldn't be dissatisfied when the first days you're trying to journal are being overwhelmed or feeling as if you're not making progress. In reality, you can see great improvement with time, but you need to get better at it. Journaling is is simple to master however, it's something that can be improved with time. The ability to put your thoughts and emotions into a form that you can read isn't an easy feat, especially when you are struggling with self-awareness.

What is Journaling? And Why is it Important?

The first thing to remember The art of journaling is not only for teenagers or children. Journaling isn't only for girls or women as well. It's something that anyone are able to connect with at any time and for anyone of any gender. It's not a thing that is restricted and you shouldn't consider it something you have to avoid or even be shamed for only because you chose to do it. In reality, journaling is an excellent practice that anyone can profit from. It's a safe space for you to document everything you think or feel out. You can keep it as private as you want it to be and as open as you like. Many people record their journals on blogs and publish them online for others to read. Some may also publish their journals in the form of an autobiography in the future. Some may still keep a journal is hidden behind their beds or hidden in an unlocked safe with keys. Whatever type of journal you keep or how open or closed you would like your journal to remain, writing is, in the first place, for you. It is a space where you are able to be able to express your feelings easily.

Journaling is important for a variety of reasons. Many people find it helpful in keeping on top of depression or anxiety. Others find it relaxing in a way that is almost ritualistic, throughout their day. The key point is to make it enjoyable, regardless of the circumstances and regardless of what you're like as an individual. Journaling can help you to record your thoughts. This will aid in understanding your personality. It is possible to identify patterns, for instance, in your thoughts, behavior or worries while you write over longer periods of time. It is also possible to connect the pieces to discover what your main worries are in your life and the reasons why you need to tackle these issues. You will begin to realize the steps required to make you better. You will be able to determine the things you really want to accomplish in life, aswell the purpose of your life. There's so much you can learn about yourself when you're watching your thoughts come into a whole before your own eyes to be able to see.

In addition to being a method to keep track of your thoughts and behavior in time, this is an ideal way to find a place where you can express your thoughts and feelings, whatever emotions you may be experiencing. Making a note of your feelings can help you to manage any emotion or stress that you don't want to shout at others. If you are writing everything down will make a safe channel that allows you to express your emotions, so you can proceed through the world. Did you get into a fight with your partner? It is possible to write over how you dislike his or her sexiness so that you don't wind with telling them something you regret. Are you feeling like you're angry with your closest friend? Write to the journal instead of telling your friend to find clarity and decide the best way to handle the situation in a rational manner instead of allowing your emotions dictate your actions. This is a fantastic and safe method for you to let your emotions out without worry. In general, however journaling can be a fantastic opportunity to gain self-awareness by reflecting on your own actions.

Self-Awareness: Why You Need It?

Let's first discover the importance of self-awareness, and why it's so crucial. This is how you begin to comprehend your own feelings, thoughts as well as your thoughts and more , by tapping into your own. Imagine this as a method of stopping, telling yourself that you're feeling something or other and become consciously aware of the feeling. We've all encountered those who aren't aware of themselves. They often think they are aware of something, but they aren't aware of how they feel at the moment or how their emotions are affecting their behavior. They could be tempted to do something they regret or was motivated by emotion without even realizing, and this can cause problems with others around them.

Self-awareness is a trait that certain people naturally possess however, others have to acquire in time. It assists you in defining your self, define the value you place on yourself as well as how you perceive yourself, and how you conduct yourself through your life. It is an extremely useful skill to have and something you'll require throughout the way you progress through it. It can help you in your relationships as you will be in a position to use your self-awareness in order to better manage your behavior. You'll be able be in control of your responses when it is the most important This means that you'll become a complete person in general.

If you don't possess a strong sense of self-awareness and awareness, there's some great news for you: you are able to build it, by taking each day as it comes by focusing on improving your capacity to pause and reflect to be sure to take the time and energy to enhance your self-awareness. Let's take a look at the ways that journaling can be one of the tools you need to use to develop self-awareness

* It aids in building the knowledge that you'll need to be able to tackle your issues efficiently.

It can help you concentrate on the things you are most focused on to help you consider the ideas you must think through to make better planned choices.

It helps you identify your priorities and the things you prioritize over other aspects.

It can help you comprehend and get clarity about your thoughts, actions and emotions

It lets you connect all of your thoughts and feelings in a larger sense so that you be aware of how the way you think and feel affects your surroundings.

The Conscious vs. The Unconscious Mind

Our thoughts take on two types: conscious and unconscious. Conscious thoughts are the ones that occur within our minds at any moment, whereas we don't know about our subconscious thoughts. While we're generally unaware of our subconscious thoughts as they occur however, we can go backwards in order to discover the nature of them over time.

This is something is typically done when you journal or self-reflection.

Journaling is when you're writing your thoughts on paper, and creating an outline of what you wrote down for later reference. While you're recording the thoughts of your conscious that you are pondering however, you're also revealing some of your personality in the process. Writing about the thoughts going through your head writing your thoughts in your head however, those thoughts can also give you details about your subconscious mind too. When you pay particular attention to the words you choose as well as sentence structure and even your handwriting when you write you'll be able gain a better understanding of the subconscious thoughts which are behind the writing.

To gain a better understanding of this concept to better understand this concept, let's consider the mind as being comprised of two distinct parts: what you know and the things you're not aware of. The mind is only aware of a small amount at any given moment in time. Your mind constantly shifts its attention from one thing to the next thing, and your awareness is restricted at any given moment. If you're interested in learning more about what's happening in your head it is important to make sure you are looking beyond your conscious awareness.

The brain that is under your conscious is the unconscious. The subconscious part of your mind is always constantly seeking to know the world around you, and constantly focused on ways to ensure that you're efficient. Imagine your subconscious mind as the background processes. Because your conscious brain is very limited, you require an approach to the things that are in your mind, but not very significant in the present. Consider, for instance how you could be able to pinpoint the exact location of something due to the fact that you have passed it even if you didn't recognize it at the time in time. Think about the way when you first begin to drive, you need to think about increasing speed and reducing speed in a conscious manner, or even how to turn your blinkers. However, as time goes on the process becomes automated. The automaticization of these behaviors was due to your unconscious mind learning how to perform it.

The subconscious mind, when exposed to something for long enough, without being challenged it will develop the habit. It will attempt to master patterns so that you do not need to think about them. This is due to the fact that you want to free the conscious mind for other tasks that require it. When traveling, it's not have be thinking about the process of getting on the pedals since it would require an excessive amount of effort. The body and your mind are taught to take shortcuts.

The issue with this but the problem is that, over time, when you experience negative thoughts that you contemplate but then dismiss your mind's unconscious, it will begin to take them in. The subconscious mind may determine that it is operating by the same set of assumptions which is why, in the end you can act these thoughts out. This is why you could create habits that later determine your behavior. It's possible that you'll be influenced by actions and thoughts that don't serve you, which could be a major issue.

If you decide to write down your thoughts for self-discovery you're trying to figure the truth about what is going on inside your mind. You're trying to unravel the thoughts that are in your head and discover the motivations that drive you. You'll examine the way that you write in order that you are able to determine the things you're passionate about. If you go back and read your writing, you'll be able look at the patterns that appear in your the language. Are you writing in a passive way? You may think of yourself as a person who is in control and all things happen to you instead of you interacting in the real world. Do you compose your writing with words that indicate that you're in control?

Journaling will allow you to identify what's happening within your own life. You'll be able to manage your life. It will allow you to overcome the suffering that you're feeling because of past traumas that could hold you back in the future, and you'll be able to tackle your unconscious thoughts to determine the best way to proceed. Journaling is one of the tools you can do to improve your self-esteem. You can utilize it to discover your identity as well as what you'd like to achieve, and so on. Journaling is a great way to explore your own inner self to discover the freedom in your mind, to improve and accept your own self. Journaling can give you the chance to connect the unconscious and conscious to help you improve yourself. You'll become the person you desire to be and writing can help you to achieve this.

## Chapter 2: Importance Of Handwriting In Your Journal

Today, in the present day it is tempting to simply write down your thoughts and thoughts. If you keep a digital journal it will be possible to access it virtually anywhereand, because of that, you'll be able take it along with you. If you you're in the mood to talk over something or something else, then you are able to do it on your phone that, nowadays users carry with them virtually everywhere they travel. You can bring it on your way for work, to school, and almost any other place, and no person will be able to tell what you're doing is recording your thoughts you're thinking about. But, despite these positives it is crucial for you to write your thoughts by hand. This book is mostly focused on the concept of writing by hand for all your journaling. If you write in hand you will notice the benefits you could miss out on in the event that you choose to create your work on a computer by typing instead.

Typing and keeping journals that are digital is much more convenient in a variety of ways. Typing is generally faster and you can record more information when you can write. In reality, the average speed related to typing is approximately forty words per minute however, the average handwriting speed is around 20. It may sound compelling in the case of someone who does not have much time in your hands however the reality is that slowing down could actually benefit your writing when it comes to your writing.

If you believe that typed and written content is the same, consider rethinking your assumptions. Writing words can be more personal, and they are more careful in what they do. It's simple to write on a computer and you can quickly fix any mistakes or typos you make, while writing far more than an average person could write. There is something satisfying with something physical, having that physically hefty hand.

We'll spend some time talking about the reasons you have to write in hand to get the best outcomes. This may sound odd at first, but believe me, the results are more personal as well as more enjoyable. It also generally yields better results over the long run. If you're going to pursue self-discovery, you'll want your thoughts laid out in front of you so that you are able to begin to pay attention to them.

Writing by hand slows you Down

If you write with a pen you're forced to slow down. However, when you are in a reflective or introspective mindset You want this. If you are able to slow down, you will have more time to slow down and reflect. This means you'll be able take the time to reflect on what you feel in greater depth. Your thoughts will seem like they are more natural once you realize that you're capable of thinking and writing simultaneously. This is good for you, and could result in writing handwritten notes that can be more honest as well as expose more of you as opposed to if you write instead. It might be uncomfortable to write with your hands but it's effective and you'll be able to consciously get across your ideas without being pressured to write something down. If you are an efficient typer and you are feeling like you need to write more often because stopping or going slow as you collect your thoughts could seem like a waste of your time and you may choose to speed up your writing. If you write with your hands it is not a issue. You will see that you're making more advancement due to being aware that your writing won't be impeded by writing by hand. When you journal with your hands rather than typing, you are able to concentrate in on the thoughts you have and emotions to sort them out. A study conducted at the University of Iowa showed positive outcomes when people decided to write their thoughts by hand on an experience that was traumatic. The journaling process was faster using a pen instead of typing, and it could have was due to being focused on the process. You must take a moment to think about each stroke while typing, however when you do so you don't have to think about that as something to worry about.

Writing with a pen and paper provides more Visual Feedback

If you write your thoughts by hand you can see the details of your mood. If you look through your journal written by hand you'll see the differences between your thoughts that are passionate as well as those that were sparked by anger. It is possible that at times they're poorly written or scattered across the paper. Feedback you receive in time is very varied from day to day and this is a reflection of the mood you were in when you composed your essay.

That means that when you write with your hands it is not just that you are making more effort to come up with those well-thought out trains of thought, but you'll be able to access additional details. The way you write is a good indicator to your feelings, which is more information that can assist you tremendously. You'll be able to make more use of your journaling due to this feedback, but this is not feasible when you choose to write instead of. Consider this: you could opt to utilize caps lock, for example, but it's not as subtle as those wavy lines you wrote when you were overwhelmed with emotion or the sharp scribble you wrote down at the midst of your anger. The pages you write on are extensions of yourself. They reflect your thoughts as well as your personality, which is crucial.

Writing by hand engages the Brain

Another aspect to take into consideration to consider is the fact that when writing with hand, you're using an totally different parts of your brain. Handwriting demands you to be thinking, manage the pen and move it in various designs across your paper. You must engage your mind in a different way as you would were, for instance, writing. This triggers a new portion of your brain and when you decide to write with your hands, instead, you utilize various parts in your mind. Writing in print, typing and writing in cursive are all different abilities, which can be extremely advantageous to you.

Handwriting by hand is proven to be more memorable. That's the reason we make notes in hand whenever we need to recall something. Sure, we could write notes on our laptops in the classroom but in reality that you'll be able to remember everything better if you've written it out by hand. Indeed, some students are known to type notes for the sake of speed , only to realize that they've handwritten them out when they are studying.

If you apply that concept to journaling too it becomes apparent that your journaling is likely be much more efficient and personal as well as more comprehensive if you choose to do it in a handwritten format instead of just typing. You'll be able better keep in mind those reflections and musings you've had in the late hours of the midnight. You'll be able more effectively utilize your reflections which is crucial. Writing by hand is a lot personalized and valuable for you. This means you'll be able to recall all the details you need.

A Physical Journal May be passed on

If you're an emotional person You might find that you're the kind of person who enjoys keeping journals that are physical due to their personal character. It is possible to pass these journals for your kids if choose to. Perhaps you're experiencing something significant that you would like to write down the thoughts you have and your feelings regarding the changes in a manner that your children are engaged too. This is what a lot of people do. You can write it down by hand and later hand it on to others if they would like to. Journals are a way to document something that you have left behind. Your computer may be damaged, and if aren't among those tech-savvy individuals who back up everything to the cloud, then you might be able to lose everything quickly and have no recourse to recover it. This can be very difficult and stressful. But, if you've got your journal in physical form You don't have these worries. Even the event that you spill water on it, depending on the ink used, it could remain legible after dry even if it's a bit wrinkled. Physical journals have a feeling of permanence that all the zeroes and ones that make up your digital journal don't have and for some it's enough to convince them to switch or change their minds.

You Can Purchase Fun Journals or Pens

Of course, what's journaling if you don't discuss the journals and pens that you'll love? If you decide to write, you have the option to choose the journal you're planning to use. Are you the type of person who is satisfied with a basic notebook that is used by students Do you feel that you're the type of person who would prefer an elegant leather-bound notebook that is stylish enough to match your style? If you write your journal in hand, you'll have an added benefit of picking the type of notebook that you believe will appeal to you.

You can also select the pen. It could be the fountain pen you prefer if like to be fancy and fancy, or you can employ a quill or ink for a pen. There's no set of rules in this case. As long as you own something that can write, it's a fair game and you are able to utilize it. It's all you have to do is be able to put the words down on paper, and ensure that you are able to read the writing. If you are able to do that then it's on the right path.

## Chapter 3: Starting To Journal

So, then, you're convinced. You're eager to begin writing in your own hand. Are you prepared? Are you prepared with the right items? A lot of people love being able to choose their own journals and pens, which was discussed in the preceding chapter. If you'd like to or you're looking to start and do not have a journal you shouldn't feel excuse not to write on a few scraps paper. You can then or write in your journal using a pen or opt to write on a piece of paper and then slip it in. Whatever you decide to do, starting is usually the most difficult aspect of the entire process. But, it doesn't need to be difficult. There are a few measures to make sure that your journaling experience is enjoyable and worthwhile to repeat. It's just a matter of knowing the process you're using.

This chapter there are some important points to consider. It is important to examine how to start a habit to write. We will talk about the importance of being consistent in journaling when you're hoping to discover yourself at the end of this process as well as the reasons why adhering to a schedule is crucial. We will also discuss the steps you must take to keep your journaling regimen In addition you'll be provided with the steps to get started.

Keep this in mind: If, for example, you have your own personal journaling routine and are just about to begin focusing on self-reflection and this is the reason you're reading this book, then you could skip this chapter. Journaling is a form of writing, and we'll get to the specifics of how to get into your thoughts and prompts you can utilize in the upcoming chapters. If you're brand new to journaling it's a good beginning point to make sure that you start off with the best possible experience. If you feel that journaling is boring or challenging, you may find yourself thinking that there's no reason to continue moving ahead in it. It might seem too complicated, too stressful or even too turgid to keep up to. But, it should be an enjoyable process for you. It must be something you appreciate and gain from. If you are finding that you don't like each and every minute of it then you may be looking to figure out how you can make it better. Journaling should be honest and not a ploy in the hopes of getting the job done.

Let's get started on addressing these issues. Once we're done here, it's the right time to begin delving into the relevant information. Even whether you're not a journalist but you can implement these habits set in place now to benefit from these. If you'd like to prove that you're an avid reporter, here's the beginning base.

How to Journal

Before we dive into a routine first let's review those essential steps to follow when journaling. The bottom line is that if you're planning to write, you have to take a seat and write down your thoughts. It is important to be able to communicate that you're keen to write down what you are thinking about right now, so that you are able to make the process of writing into the routine. Writing down your thoughts can be challenging, however. It is possible that you are stifled by the thought of writing or believe that it's something you'll never manage to succeed at. Let that thought go away today. Truth is that anyone can become an enthusiastic journalist. It doesn't require you to be a writer.

If you notice that self-doubt within your head, acknowledge the thought, then get over it and move on. It is not necessary to let it rule you. To prove that you're a journalist all you need to write about within your journals. If you'd like to to reap the benefits we've discussed so far, you must take one step: get started.

Pick up the pen and place it on your paper. Then, get writing. It's that easy. It doesn't need to be elaborate. It doesn't need become the latest best-selling novel. It's enough to create something. Anything.

If you feel like it's too much or that blank page that is in front of you seems to be too difficult to cover with ink, or you think the thoughts you've written aren't complex enough or aren't compelling enough the only thing you need to do is begin. For those who are just beginning to journal the most effective method is to simply do it and that's it. For a start, follow this simple checklist:

1. Choose your journaling tools. They can be anything as that it's the paper you want to use and a writing instrument.

2. Choose the topic you'll write about or search for an online prompt you'd prefer to take. This can give you some guidance if you are unable to figure out what you want to write about before writing about. You may even find ones that will provide you with the first word or phrase to help you get moving in the right direction If you find it too difficult to find the subject by yourself. All you need is determined to write.

3. Set a timer when you've decided on your topic. It doesn't matter for how the length you've decided to write for, it may be 5 minutes or 50 minutes. As long as you're spending time writing, it's all that matters. A good place to start for anyone who is beginning to journal is 10-15 minutes. It's not a lot of time to write your thoughts on paper. Later on, you could write more, and that's right. Don't attempt to make the

point. If all you can get at the time is just a few words then that's okay. Don't dwell. It should be natural.

4. Don't bother with editing. There is no need to be concerned about punctuation or editing. Spelling is thrown away. This is because you won't feel pressured to perfect every word you write. There's no reason to feel that you have to create the perfect draft. It's just a diary for you to have fun with, so don't attempt to complicate it.

5. Make sure to write until the alarm is set. Then, review the entire document and make any adjustments when they are needed. When you've completed this process it becomes apparent that you're able to get a good start without focusing on it , as you come back to clean the mess after. This means you could get out what you were trying to share at first, so that you could experience the most genuine, authentic emotions that you constructed, and now you see them through your words.

It's as easy as that. If you follow these steps, you will be able to eliminate the fear factor and you'll be able to continue effortlessly. All you need to do is start. It's the first time you begin will be the most difficult however, as time passes you'll notice that it becomes easier.

Beginning an Journaling Routine

Journaling involves more than simply recording your thoughts every now and there. It is a matter of getting into an established routine. To take your journaling up to the next step, and to enjoy all the benefits you're certain that you deserve it is essential to ensure that you are taking your journaling and writing to a point where it becomes regular. Since personal growth isn't something that happens in a vacuum, so you must make the effort to become comfortable with it.

If you are looking to begin with a routine, you could be concerned that it is too rigid. Remember that the plan you establish is only meant to help you get into the routine and is able to be as strict or flexible as you would like the result to be. If the schedule you set is that you create when the full moon is right above the window each month and you're happy with that, then go for it. It's up to you to decide. A lot of people want to write every day, or even every week, as they fit to their timetable. It is important to consider the amount of time you'll devote to the process of journaling in order to determine the timeframe you'd like to adhere to. If you're looking to begin your journaling regimen Then, you can come up with the followingideas:

1. Select a date and time you'd like to record your thoughts and the period you would prefer to journal during. If you'd like to write every day, then do it. If it's every other day or week you're fine too. Pick a timer and record it. It can be your first step in journaling -- to record your daily schedule and the routine you'd like to stick to. Remember that you may realize that the schedule you record may not fit your needs. If this happens then you should be flexible enough to continue trying to find out the best method for you. Do you feel that you'd like to write early in the morning but aren't able to find the motivation? Try it after

lunch or prior to going to bed. There is no way to fail or fail. The only way you could fail is to never take out the pen in the first instance.

2. Choose a relaxing pre-journaling routine. Many people feel that they work best when they have some kind of routine they utilize to become more in the mindset of a writer. Perhaps you'd prefer to drink the comfort of a cup of tea while writing or to sip the glass of wine or a glass of a good beer as you write. You might take five minutes to meditate or perhaps you have music you enjoy or take an outing to a favorite spot. There are many possibilities and you are able to pick what works for you.

3. Then, write until you're done. No matter if you set a deadline, the time limit, a writing time limit or other limitations that you set, all you need be doing is to write till you have reached the limit. This will give you a target you'll achieve that will assist you figure out what you have to do and how to complete it. Then, you're done!

When you begin do not be surprised when you realize that your emotions seem to be all over the place. It can be difficult initially however, you'll soon discover that eventually, you'll be able to make progress getting started to deal with your feelings. If you are consistent enough, you will see that you're able to manage your emotions. You'll be able to see the ways you can switch the way you behave and how you do with your own self. However, ensure that you're prepared to discover the many things you didn't even know existed within your own mind in the first place.

A few people are down when they realize their minds were filled with anxiety or fear or when their journaling sessions consistently end with a sense of negative mood. However, the truth isthat it's always best to put the negative thoughts in a notebook where they won't harm anyone. You may even discover that you are able to identify patterns you didn't even know existed at all. If you can get that negative energy out on paper, you'll be able to get away from it. It will be possible to let it go to continue to move forward in the future. It is possible some patterns you can recognize that give you the knowledge that you need to improve your life. If you are able to identify this pattern and take action you'll find that you will discover the root cause of the issue you're dealing with If you can pinpoint the cause. By identifying the source of your negative emotions, you could be able to change the things that happen to trigger them.

Maintaining a Journaling Schedule

The next step is to establish the routine that you'd like to have and then actually making journaling into a routine and habit are two distinct things. There is a possibility of creating a routine but if you don't put in your work you might not get to this stage. It is important to understand how to create a habit of writing to be capable of gaining all the advantages. The good news is that creating habits, at the very least in the abstract, isn't so difficult. It's all to repetition. If you're not willing to create this, you'll find that there are other issues which you might face instead. If you don't have the willpower to do it, you'll never develop a habit. The habit will only develop when you repeat the same behavior repeatedly.

That means you have to find a way encourage yourself and maintain the drive. Most people find that they are stuck not being able to write because they feel they're not getting anywhere or they feel like they're just not good at it and have no reason to achieve it or have other worries they face that prevent them from making progress. If you're struggling with those thoughts that make you believe that you're not able to succeed, remember that you are able to succeed, and you will so long as you set your heart into it. It's not as hard--it is simply a matter of making a decision. If you are committed and follow through your commitment, the habit will begin to form.

For this, you must ensure that you incorporate an hour or two into your day to ensure that you have the time for journaling at your disposal. Are you on an auto to work? Write, then. Do you have the same amount of time free at work? Make use of those minutes. Find an hour that is convenient for you and is feasible. Do not tell yourself that you'll write in the evening after dinner, when you have to feed the children and bathed, complete their homework, take them off to bed, and then clean up before getting yourself ready for following day. It's already a busy time. Find an hour in your day that is less occupied and use that time to be your designated journaling time. This is the most efficient method to ensure that you take time to sit down each day.

Remember that having smaller isn't always a bad thing. If you're not able to devote 20 minutes to write every day every day you can do that. If all you have is five minutes between chores then that's fine as well. All you have to do is begin to do it. Remember that just five minutes is more important than nothing. If you truly want to commit, then you must to make the most of it feasible to achieve success.

Last but not least, remember that you're not like the same as other people. It is not a good idea to try to adhere in the same way other people follow. That's why Suzie next door shared via social networks about writing four pages of her journal on the day she posted it. You're not Suzie. You're not a failure simply because that you composed a sentence prior to concluding that you're done. Journaling is a personal experience. It's for you and not for anyone else. Don't get caught up with what others think, when their thoughts don't really matter to you. It's not necessary to worry about them, you need to be concerned about yourself.

## Chapter 4: Recording Your Goals

What do you envision yourself doing in 10 years? Do you think you would like to make it there? If not, what is the reason? If yes, how do you achieve it?

These are all connected to the goals. Every person has goals in our lives whether it's paying the bills, or relocate to a new country, or even to start an enterprise or family. Each of us has a different goal to consider that we can use to propel ourselves ahead, and that's wonderful! But, they can seem elusive and hard in some instances. They can also be difficult to attain when you aren't sure the process or how to make goals that are achievable. Many times, people tend to set goals that are difficult to make come to fruition. They make goals believing that they're meant to be difficult and even though they're supposed to be stretching, and that you must be able to work towards them however, there isn't a rule which says they must be considered as putting your life in high-stress mode. Actually it is exactly the opposite. Your goals should be achievable. They must be achievable so that you don't creating a risk for failing, which all often do, without realizing they are doing it. In reality, many people aren't able to set goals and they end up failing to sabotage the whole process. If you're hoping to achieve success it is essential to understand how to establish your goals.

The next chapter we're going to be talking about goals and the reasons they are important. We will explore the way they are created to be successful to help you attain them and also the steps to take to make sure they are formulated to allow you to follow them in a way that is effective. Goals are tools you must be able to utilize towards your goals of success in life. They shouldn't be a burden or difficult to implement. They must be something can be beneficial to you to be certain of success in your career. They should guide you, not be the cause of conflict.

Journaling is one method to start to determine what your objectives in life could be. It is possible to look at how you write in order to start to determine what you would like to achieve the most. Also, we will look at the ways you can use this idea and the notes that you record while journaling to help you begin to recognize the values you hold dear to your heart. This is crucial for you because it is the first step in identifying the things you value that is the start of self-awareness. Once you are able to pinpoint your goals and then recognize them you can begin to determine how you're approaching your objectives in a manner that's likely to succeed.

What Are Your Goals?

The first step is to take the time to determine what your objectives you want to achieve and the reasons why they are important to define goals. The truth is that when you don't have goals laid out in front of you so that you can be able to see them, there's an excellent possibility that you'll have randomly try to attain what you desire, but you're never likely to get the place you'd like to be. Consider this: What is the scenario if you've decided you're planning to take a trip out to dinner this evening? You decide, "I'm going out for dinner tonight." You hop in the car, and begin driving. It's a completely new place and unknown, and you don't have the luxury of driving to the restaurant you've identified as the one you're looking for. There's a chance that you didn't have a specific restaurant in your mind at all. You don't even have your mobile phone on your, and there's no means of looking for it and determine where to go. What can you do?

You can go around in circles and pray that you find an establishment that sells foods... However, it could end up being a complete waste of time both literally and metaphorically, when you're unlucky enough to are located far from where you'd want to find the restaurant in the first instance. You could get confused and not knowing what brought you to where you have ended up in the first instance.

A lack of a plan in life, or having a goal that's properly formulated is like being the person who is hungry and lost with no route to get from A to B. It's exhausting and tiring and frequently difficult and unpleasant. It is possible to be lucky in the process And, yes, sometimes you may end up in a place you never desired to go however the reality is that most times you'll end up dissatisfied. That's why goals are important.

A goal is a defined purpose you've set. It must be closed-ended to ensure you can be sure there's something that is a sign of success or failure. They must also be achievable. If you want to construct a rocket that can carry into space but you're not a rocket scientist, knowledge of engineering or math, how can you expect to accomplish this? The idea that you'd build it is extremely unlikely unless the motivation for the aim is going to college for research in rocket sciences, or even for that matter. in the first place.

The goals we set are to help us apply and gain meaning from our lives. They give us direction to ensure that we achieve what we desire to. They're there in order to help us understand them into pieces so we can comprehend the steps we'll have to follow to go from which is where we are at the beginning and to reach point B successful, with as little hiccups as feasible.

Goals are set because they have the ability to control their own lives. The pace of life is hectic and it's easy to drift away from what you ought to be doing. But the fact is, if spend the time to think about it to consider the options, you can determine ways to get you back to where you want to be or would like to be. The goal setting process serves a variety of goals for you. They may:

• Help you focus where you're required to be In the event that you are capable of defining what you're looking to accomplish and what you must accomplish, along with the time frame you've set and your goals can assist you get the best possible outcome. The goal you set can be your ability to determine the steps required for you to accomplish the things you want to do, and this is extremely useful to you. When you have a goal in mind, you'll be creating the conditions to become the most successful person you are able to be.

They will help you get your bearings Help you determine what exactly it is that you are looking for and what you want to be. They will assist you in getting there, which means you'll be better able to manage your time, yourself and your effort because you'll be guided by them.

Making New Goals

Setting new goals can be somewhat daunting However, the reality is that it's extremely easy if you have the proper structure. To start putting together your goal, you should be aware of what you're looking for to achieve in the first place. We'll get to this in the following section. In the meantime we'll assume that if you're going to establish goals, you have made the effort to record your thoughts and come up with the things you'd like to get the most of your life. We'll assume that you know the way you'd like to achieve this end goal and you know the outcome.

Consider that you would like to purchase an apartment. This is the goal--you're saying that you would like to have your own house. It's a sensible target. Many people are striving for, even though it's admittedly difficult dependent on your financial situation are in. If you're looking to reach your goal you must make a plan. You require a method by which you will be able to begin to determine the things you will be doing in order that you are able to more effectively direct your actions. Simply saying you'd like to buy a home is like saying you'd like to go from point A to the point B. It is important to determine the steps needed to take to get there. One of the most effective ways to achieve this is the development of goals that are SMART. It is an acronym meaning:

* Specific

* Measurable

* Realisable

* Realism

* Timed

If you adhere to this template to achieve your goals, you will be able to ensure that you complete all the steps necessary to bring you to where you're getting to and help you get to that point of happiness throughout your daily life. Just take the time to complete the gaps and you'll be able to discover it. Let's examine each step in detail so that you are able to gain a better understanding of the process.

Specific

The first step is to be aware that the most effective objectives can be the most precise. These are the goals which will help you figure out the direction you should be and allow you to arrive at your destination quickly because you know precisely where you're going. Imagine an example of the distinction between "I would like to go to the restaurant" to "I would like have dinner at Johnny's Diner." If you have the precise image painted it is clear that you're headed to somewhere particular. This means that there's more room for error and less chance of getting lost and that's extremely essential. The goal should always be as specific as it is possible. Consider the various factors that go into the two scenarios: you want savings, and would like to save $20,000 as a down payment for the home you've always wanted. When you declare that you have this amount in your head, you will know that you have the capacity to establish a strategy. You will have a limited end date, and that's what you require here to reach a satisfactory target. It is difficult to achieve open-ended goals because there isn't an end-to-end explanation so you don't have a way to know if and when you've succeeded or have failed.

Measurable

Then, you need to ensure that the goal that you've set in your the mind can be measured. Your goal must be quantifiable to ensure that on the way, it is possible to monitor your improvement. This is crucial to achievement because if you are aware that you're in the wrong or correct path, you are able to change your course should they be required. If you have clear plans in your mind, and knowing the distance you're from being successful, you'll be able follow your goals more closely. Most of the time the information you find here is an opportunity to breakdown your goals for you. If you are able to quantify that down payment, it's probably in cash since cash is the best method of evaluating your progress towards achieving the goal of cash. If you're trying to make $20,000 savings, you may consider yourself half way there when you deposit the first $10,000 into your bank account, and claim that you're 1 percent of the way there when you deposit your first $200. By determining your goals, you begin creating increments you can utilize.

Attainable

The following point is that your objective needs be achievable. Are you able to accomplish this goal? can do? Consider the ways you could determine to fly with no kind of equipment. Is this feasible for us? If you don't have any kind of mechanism to create wings or to lift off it, this isn't possible for human beings and is therefore not feasible. But other goals, like building a house might be feasible when you're working. If the goal could be at least in some manner, form or form, achievable that is, then it's doable. If not, it's time to go back to the beginning and come up with a new idea.

Realistic

Realistic is quite more than achievable. Certain goals are achievable but they aren't realistic. For instance, what happens if you make a goal of running 10 minutes to cover a mile? Yes, it is possible in the event that there aren't any physical issues that hinder you from doing it. But is it really feasible? Are you really willing to take this step? If you desire to take on the challenge but are you sure it would be a real challenge for you? If you're already able to run in a 10 minute mile it is not a good need to consider it as your goal or unless it's that involves running a mile each day to keep healthy or isn't related to speed. Being realistic as a quality to achieve your goal is about helping you make sure that the goals are relevant to you. If you are able to possibly save money in the future, however, in reality you're red-lining each month for a minimum of $300, making a savings of $300 every month might not be something you could use towards an down payment as an example. If this is attainable your situation, proceed. If not, contemplate what you can do to make it more real, or alter your plans completely. If your goal is achievable it is important to be sure to specify what it is. For instance, if you are looking for a savings of $20,000 you can declare that you'll accomplish this by putting aside $1,000 per month, to ensure that in two years, you'll have the money.

Timed

The final aspect to take into consideration is what the deadline for it is. Your goal shouldn't be undefined, otherwise there will never be the possibility of failing. It is essential to ensure there's a point of failure, so you aren't able to delay your progress and convince yourself that you're actually doing your best to achieve your goal but actually, you're not. This is a major issue that many individuals face and is a real challenge to overcome. It's the matter of setting some kind of end-point in which you state that you've been successful or not.

Writing about Your Goals

If you are trying to figure out your goals and then determining your goals, the most effective method is to understand yourself more. Consider what it is that you'd like to accomplish. Make a list of your priorities and hopes for the future. If you take this approach you'll realize that you have a greater chances of success by being in a position to determine the goals you want to achieve first.

It may be a challenge But keep this in mind: You're considerably more likely to reach your goals if you record them down. If you're looking to know your goals Write down your expectations. Answer the questions mentioned above. Are you looking to have children? If yes, what are the steps you have to do in order to make that happen? The things you require to accomplish whatever it is that you want will assist you greatly if know the reasons behind them and the best way to achieve them. That means that you should be looking within at yourself.

If you've been writing review the things you've written. How often have you spoken in regards to the near future? What are the times you've said that you were waiting for something to occur? This might give an insight into your objectives. If you're still not sure then, take a look at the steps given below.

Journaling Prompt 1

Take a moment to think about the ideal lifestyle you would like to live. Consider your current location and what you do and how you live your life. Spend some time to picture this in your mind and think of each detail as in the depth you can. After that, record your day as though you had lived it. Be sure to record your actions as well as what you wished to accomplish, and much more. And then, think about what it would take to get you to reach this position in the first place.

This question will allow you see what it is you truly want from life and the things you are most proud of. It could be that you've opted for an individual kind of lifestyle like one who is been focused on their career as well as volunteering, the church, even the family. It can provide you with valuable insight into what you value most. You can then begin thinking about what you'd have to do in order to reach that point at all.

Journaling Prompt 2

What is your definition of an exemplary life?

This simple question is more specific than the previous but is also much more flexible. It lets you stop and think about the various things that you think are indicative of your success. These is likely to be carried over to your present life too.

Journaling Prompt 3

If you could do just one thing that you could do with no money the only factor (either because you need to pay for your hobby or because you need to pay for living expenses , and thus you never had to work again to make ends meet) What would you do? Why?

This will allow you highlight your beliefs. If you're an individual who has decided to keep animals for your family You may discover that this is your main ambition. It is possible that you'd like to build homes or compose music or write books, without having to worry about selling them. This is an excellent opportunity to look at what your real desires in life are.

Journaling Prompt 4

What was the biggest dream you dreamed of as young? What were your goals to be when you grew up? Are you there today, or have you realized that these values don't matter anymore to you? Take a moment to think about this and write your thoughts down.

This prompt will show you the way your thoughts have evolved throughout time and if you've ever found that bliss in your life. It can also help to recall the things you were most proud of in the past, and the way you feel about at the moment.

## Chapter 5: Do Not Give Up And Keep Focused On The Goal

If you want to be successful to be successful, you have to keep moving forward and concentrate on the rewards that await you when you reach the end. Sometimes, it are so difficult that the only option is to quit and go back to how things were. Don't be affected by pressure , because If you do, your entire life is going to be nothing. Your efforts will go to waste and your desire to connect to your soul will disappear.

It's not just you person who experiences this Everyone who chose to take on the process of self-discovery was through the same things you are experiencing right now and others may even be in more trouble than you do. Your experience isn't the most severe but it won't be the easiest one to manage either.

Do what you've been doing all along and let go of the negative comments as you're close to self-discovery and concentrate on achieving your goal.

Procrastination Is An Evil Word

You've made that you're going to begin an adventure of self-discovery Do not put it off until the next day. If you do, it will result in you losing the initial excitement or enthusiasm and could even put you off before you even begin. It is incredibly easy to pull you away from your plans . Don't let it happen.

Once you've decided to go on the road ensure that you complete your schedule with no delay. Keep in mind that putting off your plan isn't the best way to start, and it is a high likelihood that you won't begin something in the first place.

Organise and Simplify

The benefit of being simple is that everything is simple to understand and doesn't require many steps to complete tasks. If everything is well-organized and the process isn't too difficult for you to understand, you'll be able to follow the plan and be able to begin any time immediately and immediately.

It is important to organize or plan everything to make your trip an enjoyable one, despite the obstacles you must overcome.

Remove Negativity

Negative thinking can only bring you down. If you believe that you'll fall short before the process even begins and you think that you'll fail, then you'll. Your brain is already feeding your body with things that are not useful and instead of providing motivation and motivation, it causes you to derail the whole process. This could cause you to give up on the idea altogether and accept the situation as it is even though you could improve your self.

The Objectives May Not be Easy To Achieve

You're trying to achieve the same goal, but you must be prepared to take on any challenge and accept the possibility that it could be more difficult than you anticipated. There are many different people with different circumstances and the achievement of their goals may not occur within the same period of time. Maintain a steady and consistent attitude always, as these are essential in the event that you're truly determined to achieve your goals. Prepare yourself for the worst, and always believe in the most favorable outcome.

There is no way to say that Man is an Island You Can Rely on Your Loved Ones More

Knowing that you're not on your own in this endeavor will make the process easier and easier to handle. You can rely more on the people you trust, including your family and friends, to provide you with more motivation and motivation to continue and never quit. Their encouragement words or their presence can keep you focused on completing the initial goal.

Don't give up halfway

Yes, there are instances when the most effective option to choose is to abandon and come back but do you truly believe you will become the person you truly deserve to become should you turn back? For the record you won't achieve your full potential if take that route and you'll never be in a position to let your true self show through.

Don't give up halfway and if you've been the ability to get this far, then the second half that's going to take you to your destination isn't too difficult to attain. It's easier today opposed to the days when you just started. Consider the rewards you'll earn and keep going.

## Chapter 6: Arduous Yet Nevertheless Worthy Path To Take

Now is the time to tackle serious business. If you're prepared to go on upon the journey of the rest of your life. Relax and you'll soon be able to identify what you need to accomplish to reconnect with your own inner self.

Your Old Definition

It is known that your brain makes a label through definition by analysis. Everything that you're experiencing right now have been identified by your brain. the label you currently are wearing is the definition you have.

Start writing down your personal definition of yourself by listing your name age or gender, work fear or phobia and hobbies, likes and dislikes, habits you are aware of, your addictions, past times or friends, and anything else that you think has made an effect and helped you become the person you are now. It is possible to include whether or not you excel at athletics or are not. You can also include whether you possess a weak bones, isn't great in school or studying, and other such things.

The labels you've just given to yourself will become your original definition once you begin to let go of the labels that are not favorable either improve them or keep the positive things in mind to come up with a new definition and connect to your self-image.

Doubt is a good thing when it's doubtful.

Each label you're given, take a step back and determine if this is the one you actually have for yourself. Does the person you are labeled the one you hoped to be, or is it simply a definition that you've always believed in due to the fact that you were destined to believe in it?

Be skeptical about the definitions you've written down, and determine whether the label is an accurate picture of you or something you've accepted as a fact because nobody said to you to doubt it. Doubting at this point is good however you should be doubting your thinking. Be sure not to question the meaning that allows your inner self shine. If you are convinced that the definition fits you perfectly, then let it remain. If not, then you should either throw it away the definition or create something that makes your inner self shine.

Believing In The Benefits

After you have sorted the labels to take into consideration, you should ask yourself whether the labels are useful to your goal and development. You'll need to be able to trust your gut, and be attentive to its whims. It is your own inner voice reaching towards you, slowly but gradually.

Meditation can aid in this process and will awaken your senses and help you evaluate things more accurately. Follow your instincts and develop a new meaning that you are happy to live by.

Making an alternative definition

The best thing you could make with definitions or labels that have no benefit for you is to develop an alternative. Instead of saying that you're an avid drinker, consider saying you are an occasional drinker. Instead of saying that you're a quitter, try being the label of an addict to see if you can take on a challenge. In short, come up with an ideal definition of what you wish to be and ensure that you adhere to your new idea to be accurate.

Make a mantra that you repeat repeatedly until you're the ability to train your brain to adhere to the phrase. You could declare, "I have always been an (insert below the term that you would like to replace) and I'm now going to quit and transform into (insert this definition you would like to be identified with).

It is possible to claim, "I have always been one to give up and I'm going to put it all behind and turn into addicted to a test".

The whole process could cause you to feel as if you're cheating yourself, but that's the price you must pay to change things around. Don't accept your new definition, and stick to the new definitions (and be patient with the process) This whole process typically takes a minimum of 30 months before the brand new one can sink into.

You may feel that you're living in a fake persona when you repeat the definition over and over again to yourself. After that testing, your subconscious has recognized your new identity as your true self so everything flows effortlessly. You've connected to your own self, but it does not end there. It is essential to ensure that you are in complete control over your true self and not let it go.

As time passes, you may be tempted to do a self-reflection, but this time, to enhance areas that require improvements. This can make you stronger and more efficient. You redefine yourself in order to adjust to the changing needs of the society. You must grow as society improves. It is possible that you will need to redefine your current status to keep up with evolving times.

## Chapter 7: Writing To Control Emotions

The ability to regulate emotions is among the most essential skills can be learned by anyone. It's vital that we put a lot of effort on it with our children, attempting to show the skills they need to become more balanced, more productive, and better at solving negative emotions. How often do we find ourselves talking to kids about their current moodto determine how they feel? This is done because being capable of preventing yourself from being a victim of your emotions is essential. It's adorable when a toddler cries and screams, but it's a bit gruelling and offensive when an adult is doing it. We must learn to regulate ourselves, and manage our emotions in the end.

Of of course, some live our lives without mastering these techniques. We do not know the steps needed to know how we can manage our emotions which is a major issue. But, like any skill, you can master this anytime. Don't think you're lost even if you don't possess the right skills for managing your emotions. You are able to learn it with a bit of patience, a little work, and some traditional journaling.

## Self-Regulation and managing your emotions

The ability to manage your emotions is the capacity to regulate how you react to the situation you're in. It's about being able to identify what you must do to avoid being a victim of certain behaviors and then overcoming these. Imagine that you did not get the job that you had been interviewing for. It's a normal feeling to be disappointed and nobody can blame you for it. Imagine that you left the room crying and ranting about how unfair life is and that you were not worthy of the position. This would be considered to be excessive, according to the majority of people. This kind of behaviour is unacceptably and is a matter you must address. There is no reason to accept this kind of attitude from a mature adult, and with a valid reason it is not appropriate for anyone over the age of school to be running around complaining about injustice.

When you master the art of managing the emotions you experience, they aren't taught to shut them down to the darkest and most dark corners of your brain. Instead, you strive to make sure you are controlled in other ways. It is possible to make sure that your behavior is better managed by learning how to self-regulate. Self-regulation is a crucial aspect of successful people. It is one of the most important aspects of emotional intelligence, as well as other related skills to work effectively throughout the course of life.

Self-regulation is the ability to control your emotions at any time because you know the state of mind the moment is. It involves controlling emotions, thoughts and behaviours to ensure that you're acting in ways that are positive. It can also positively impact other areas that you live. It's how we handle stressful situations and can help us establish the basis of our relationship, behavior and, in the end our success. The people who can perform well, via self-regulation can control their stress more effectively. They generally feel happier and more likely to act in ways that are going help not only them but their family and friends too. Self-regulation can be simple however, it is vital.

People who have a knack for self-control can gain in a variety of ways, for example, being able to appreciate traits like:

Believing in their beliefs: Those who are self-regulatory know that they shouldn't sacrifice their joy to other people. They remain true to their beliefs so that they don't think that they sacrificed their integrity to other people or objects.

* being able to settle when stressed and be positive when you're feeling down: People who are self-regulating experts know they're competent in helping themselves be calm when they're overwhelmed by negative emotions. Whatever the cause, whether it is about the way they behave or not they can improve their self-control and as a result they are aware that they're able to perform better. In addition, they're in a position to feel more relaxed when they are upset over something else as well.

Communication with others: People who have mastered self-regulation are aware of how important it is to influence their actions. They know that, ultimately they should be sure to express themselves regardless of negative feelings they may experience.

Persisting through moments of difficulty Being able to mentally manage yourself will help you keep your focus on not giving up even when circumstances get tough.

Being flexible The most effective emotional regulators can manage their emotions when they notice that things shift. They are able to handle the change in stride in order to grow.

• Optimism emotion regulators always discern the good for a situation as well as others, even though there are people who are troublesome also.

The ability to develop self-regulation of your emotions as you will see, is crucially important. It is essential to know how to use it in order for success. For children this can be created through routines and expectations which allow them to know what to anticipate, when to anticipate it, and the reasons to anticipate it. This helps them feel more at ease and are able to perform better for themselves and others. As time passes, it becomes the self-regulation they require.

As adults it's more complex. You don't have a family member standing by your side and helping you through each step of the way , if you're not yet familiar with the basics. You can, however, be able to learn how to do it by yourself. The first step to doing so is to acknowledge that, like everyone else has a choice. The decision you make is not dependent on others but on you. Your decision to make is contingent on the way you choose to control your own behavior around others. When you realize that and realize that in the end you are in control of your own behavior, and you begin to realize the results that you've been looking for.

When it comes to circumstances in your life, you have three choices. You have the option of reacting at the events around you by utilizing these methods. You can decide to tackle the situation with a straight face, which will allow you to be closer to the issue in the hopes of solving it. You can also avoid it by as if it didn't exist and everything are fine in the absence of acknowledging the things that are taking place around you. It is also possible to confront the situation, becoming aggressive and defensive about it. When you react to a situation it is categorized into the three categories. Although it may seem like you aren't in control but the reality is that you're in total control of the situation. You are able to alter the way you behave and, while your feelings affect this decision but you also be the ultimate decision maker on the matter.

After you have realized that you are in control of the situation The next step towards self-regulation is to be conscious of the emotions that are passing by. What do you want to do when you are in a state of emotion? What do you'd like to do if you're faced with the challenge of a situation? Are you looking to flee away, or do wish to take on the person you thought of as having wronged you? It is important to know where you stand on this issue so that you can begin to manage the issue and also. Be aware of your emotions when you feel them within your body. Do you feel that you are hurting somebody? Are you looking to change your behavior? What motivates you to alter your behavior? Determine the cause to begin to control your behavior. By being able to comprehend your physical and emotional state of mind and body, you will be able to begin to manage yourself well.

Utilizing Journaling to manage your Emotions

If you are considering journaling to help you manage your emotions, you're opting to improve your life using very precise techniques. The seven stages to emotional control, and through journaling you can tackle 5 of these. These steps to address emotionality are:

* Making space between yourself and your feelings

* Define emotions

* Releasing and releasing emotional tension

* Concentrating on powerful emotions

* Organizing your mind to clear emotions

* Regrouping after emotional events

* Keeping up with the abilities

Of these skills that are all about focusing on emotional turmoil and keeping your skills up to date can be dealt with by writing. You can assist yourself in learning to get away from you and your feelings by taking a look at your feelings towards the emotions you experience at all. Learn to manage these feelings in order to manage them throughout time. You can identify your emotions, work to discover what they mean and identify them by writing in your journals and journals. You may decide to let go your emotions by write about them. You can also decide to arrange your thoughts by analyzing your thoughts so you are able to better understand your own thoughts. It is also possible to improve yourself by reorganizing when you've experienced emotional traumas, too. This happens due to the manner you choose to handle the circumstances you're facing, and the faster that you can come to terms with the manner that things unfold the faster you will be able to improve your own self as well.

When you write to deal with your feelings the best method to get started is to focus on one of the five aspects listed before this. If you can identify these, you'll see that eventually, you will be able to see progress and make the transition towards being more in control of your emotions your own emotions.

Journaling Prompt 1: Freewrite

The first prompt. Write for 15 minutes, without stopping to edit or revise your writing. It is just writing for 15 minutes and not stop even if your writing "I am not sure what I thought," or "I'm not certain of what else to write about." More often you practice this the better it becomes.

For the first prompt for freewriting be sure to take a moment and think about the lowest point in your day of today. What made the situation so difficult, and what would you wish you could do differently to make it more manageable?

Through freewriting, you're writing down all of your internal thoughts. This can assist you understand the thoughts you've been relying on. It can help you know the depth of the feelings you are experiencing to better deal with them on your own.

Journaling Prompt 2

Consider something difficult to tackle now and think about what you you would have told yourself at that moment. Now you know how things will unfold. Do you wish you could have changed the way you dealt with the issue initially? What is the reason? What do you think of the current situation now that it's ended?

This prompt is intended to stimulate you to think about the other emotions you might be dealing with, so you can be sure that you will enhance your life in the near future. The more proficient you become in controlling your emotions and feelings, the better you'll get in controlling the whole thing.

Journaling Prompt 3

Sit down for a while and imagining the ideal day that you can live. Imagine that you didn't have any restrictions, no obligations and all the funds needed to complete a task. What would you do? Imagine a perfect day and then record it. Think about what you felt like while writing about the perfect day. You can take a moment to reflect on the day. What was it that made that day so the perfect day? What is the reason you would like to accomplish that particular task?

This prompt can be used for two purposes: it allows you to feel connected to your positive feelings , and also works on your visual skills in addition to helping you create a visualisation that you can to apply to help yourself. The visualization can be something you can use anytime you feel stressed, emotional or overwhelmed. If you feel that your anxieties or worries are beginning to get all over you You can go of that image to use it to help in the regulation process.

Journaling Prompt 4

Every person experiences emotions at various points in the present, and these emotions aren't always easy to define in the absence of knowing what we're doing or how we can do it. Sit down and consider the emotions you are experiencing and try your best to understand them. Spend as long as you can thinking about what you feel and why it is and what you could do accomplish to change it. Write as detailed as you can, what you are feeling and the way those feelings affect you. Next, you can assign an end to the emotion.

This prompt is intended to force you to slow down and reflect on what your emotions feel like. It also will require you to sit down and think about the feelings, emotions, and the emotional reaction you experience as a result. You must be able to define your physical sensations as well as the way that those physical sensations affect you react to the circumstances.

## Chapter 8: Writing To Determine Emotional Triggers

They are unpredictable, and they do not happen in an isolated bubble. The emotions you experience generally trigger something, and there is an external influence at work creating the emotional response. But the fact that you are experiencing an emotional trigger, it doesn't mean that you are given free rein to act as if you're not responsible for the reactions you have whenever you experience an intense emotion. It is true that you must acknowledge the triggers that trigger your emotions and then own for the emotions you are experiencing. Keep in mind that you have control over your own behavior at all times, whether you think that or not. If you're looking to improve your self-esteem, the first place is to consider how you react to the world around you.

The emotional triggers can be difficult to grasp at times. this is why we're going to take some time examining the nature of these triggers and how they can affect you, as well in how you can begin to pinpoint triggers so you can begin to fix the issue. As time passes, you'll discover that you've got the ability to overcome these triggers, and to detach them to not trigger your reactions. You can control yourself , even when triggers are in play by enticement, provoking, and convincing you to react to them. If you take a look at your triggers for emotional reactions and learn to recognize them, you'll be able start improving yourself. Then you'll have the ability to begin working towards control of your own emotions and the ones which you're dealing with in order to improve your control and also.

What are Triggers?

Emotional triggers are subjects, events or actions that instantly cause a visceral, intense response to something. The visceral reaction may be a feeling of sadness, anxiety or ashamed, or outraged. This can cause you to feel more powerful than you think they would and you could get extremely reactive at that point too. It's the feeling of making a joke, and the feeling of being unhappy or embarrassed throughout the day. There are many emotional triggers, which are usually related to emotional trauma that we have carried from our past. everyone has to figure out how to move past it at some point or some other point. If you're capable of identifying what the triggers are that you face and then you can begin to address these triggers.

The triggers you experience are usually triggered by experiencing pain you couldn't manage when you were a kid. Your body or your mind were not equipped to deal with what occurred to you, so instead of being in a position deal with everything, you deliberately suppressed it in order to not deal with the issue. It is then that you forget about the issues were once yours until you're reminded by these issues.

The trigger is that reminder. It can bring your mind back to where it was before and, as a consequence you are more immersed in your feelings. You are feeling like this child all over again, suffering and scared but you aren't sure how to stop such emotions from happening at all. These triggers are yours to deal with in the beginning so that you don't become dependent on them. But, if you are able to manage those triggers you'll be able beat them and overcome the impact they exert on you.

If you're not able to manage these triggers, you'll likely realize that your emotions remain stuck incapable of overcoming these triggers. When you discover an avenue to grow by overcoming the triggers, you'll find that they're not as difficult to overcome as you believed. However, getting to this point may require some effort. Let's examine some of the more frequent triggers people encounter before moving on to being able identify them.

* Rejection: Maybe you had parents absent or were abandoned or disapproved of by your parent. Or maybe you had friends who frequently disengaged from you and had no interest in you whatsoever. Whatever the reason, rejection can make you feel anguish, guilt, anger or even anxiety.

A feeling of helplessness over something As an infant, you experienced events that were not your control and caused harm and/or traumatizing or challenging to confront and you are feeling overwhelmed when you face situations you are not able to manage.

The feeling of being ignored Particularly when you had parents who did not pay attention towards you. You may discover that being ignored can be an enormous emotion trigger. If you notice that someone doesn't listen to your voice and suddenly triggers you it could be because of this reason.

Someone who is not reachable or unresponsive: Sometimes it's just the fact that someone is inaccessible, even for a short period and that's the issue for you. If you begin to feel shivering when you realize you aren't able to get hold of another person, and you immediately consider the the worst-case scenario.

* Someone looks at you in a negative way This can be particularly prevalent with parents who are extremely critical. They tend to be judgmental and despise more than any other thing, and it could cause major issues for the child.

* Someone who is insecure or sexually intimate with you: This can be due to all kinds of reasons, including the fear of commitment, or perhaps an alleged past history of abuse sexual of some type.

* Someone who is controlling you: If someone else tries to dictate what you what you should do something, you may be feeling as if you're being held under their wing, feeling uneasy and in a bind.

Of of course, these are only some of the many types of triggers available. It is possible the trigger to be someone who appears like a certain way, or an expression somebody else said or similar. In reality, anything can trigger someone if they did it in the right manner which means that you'll need to learn to handle those situations as time passes. You'll need to understand how you can improve your own skills and avoid that issue from happening again from occurring again.

The first step towards healing is to recognize and identify the trigger areas. When you have figured out the triggers that set your body off, you can begin to resolve the issue completely. This is something which requires effort and energy, but with time, you'll be able how to conquer it. Remember that you are the only one competent of resolving your triggers. Only you can restore yourself and bring your self back to the level of being productive. If you are looking to reach the point at which you are, then you'll need to think about the triggers that cause you to act what triggers you, the reason why it matters and what you can do to begin to eliminate the triggers that you engage in. Keep in mind that this is something that takes time. It isn't enough to just try to conquer your triggers without thinking about it. You have to commit yourself to start to address the issue.

Utilizing Journaling to Determine Your Triggers

Journaling can provide you with the possibility of knowing your triggers. If you're in the correct direction, it is possible to begin to write with the intention of helping you discover the emotions you experience in order to reduce them to the point where they are not affecting your life anymore. It is possible to overcome the issue so that you are able to improve and be able to take control of your emotions.

If you are looking to pinpoint what triggers you are experiencing, the most effective method to do this is to create a an outline of the things you experience throughout the day. You can then create your own daily journal of everything that you feel, the occurred in relation to those feelings and how you can address your current situation. Once you've got the log, you'll begin to identify patterns to identify what the actual trigger is.

The first step in using journaling to pinpoint what triggers you is to ensure you know what triggers are. This means that you should begin recording your feelings when you feel them throughout your day. Although it's generally good to keep track of all emotions in order to be concise we'll look only on the emotions that are negative you feel. We'll look at how the negative emotions which you are experiencing will impact your life, and the way your surroundings influence these negative feelings. Over a time, until you've discovered the pattern, you should begin to record all emotions. Each time you experience an outburst, you are experiencing, keep the following notes to yourself:

* What's the feeling I'm having?

* What caused these emotions?

* What time is it?

* Where was I when I left

* Who was the person who was involved?

How did I feel prior to the event?

Once you have all of this written down, you are able to search for patterns. Perhaps you notice that you are always snappy throughout the day , even before lunchtime. There may be something for you to investigate to determine the reason why this happens at all.

Once you've got everything written down, it's the time to start searching for reasons that lead you to find yourself feeling the way you do. You'll need to address your feelings in a direct manner, however that implies that you must discover the source of them first. it will take some the time and effort. Find out what matters to you. Continue to inquire about why they were important for you till you can pinpoint the root cause of the issue. Sometimes, it's buried somewhere deep in the ground however, you can locate it by searching until you find the truth. It could take a while but you are able to do it.

By retrospection, you'll begin to understand the reason these feelings matter to you. You may find that the truth of the situation is that you're dissatisfied with the way you feel about something that has transpired. It is possible that you have unresolved emotions from your childhood that are weighing on your mind or perhaps you think that there's no way to escape the feeling of being trapped by the people that surrounds you. Whatever the circumstance however, you will discover the way to healing.

When you are aware of the triggers that you are experiencing and what triggers you are, it is time to be proactive. You can begin to think about the reason why these triggers are there initially and then try to determine how you can avoid them through your reflections on yourself. In time, as you become aware of your own feelings and thoughts more deeply, you'll realize that you do have total control over your emotions. You'll discover that you're the only one who is able to control what you feel, how is happening, as well as how you feel this way. Your trigger could stem from an unresolved trauma you experienced when you were a kid, but you're no longer the child you were. You're a mature adult with the ability to solve the issues you face by yourself. You no longer need help. are the power you desire over yourself, and you are able to decide to take it on when you know the right thing to do.

You can start to confront your triggers. You can determine what you're going to do to overcome them, and you can begin to work with yourself to avoid becoming sensitive in the first instance. You can convince yourself that there's no reason to get so obsessed with those emotions. You can work towards reducing the sensitivity of yourself until you are able to see the root of the issue.

Journaling Prompt 1: Trigger Tracker

The first prompt for journaling could be more of an assignment rather than a journal entry However, it's vital in helping you. This prompt requires you'll need to dedicate a week to documenting the emotional reactions you are experiencing. You're looking for clues to the state of your emotional life is at any given point in time, and begin to record the moment you realize it is spiraling. If you are feeling intensely that you're feeling angry, hurt or in any other way emotionally intense You must take a break and write it down whenever you get the opportunity. Note in your diary the day and time at which the incident took place. It is important to note the emotion you felt was. You should record information about your surroundings, the people who live there, and the background of the emotions you experienced. It should be done for at least a week , so you will be able to search for patterns.

This is crucial because it will help you begin recording the emotions you feel when you are experiencing them. This is the initial step in learning to manage them before they control you.

Writing Prompt #2: Five Reasons

This prompt is straightforward The next task is simple: Pick one of the events you wrote about in your initial journal, and examine the situation. The aim here is to identify the five reasons for the issue you encountered. You're looking for details regarding the reasons it is that way you do in order that you can get over it. You're trying to write down your feelings the way you did, reasons why you felt this way,. This is done by asking yourself why you felt the way you did. You want to determine what the significance of this situation is to you. First, you must identify the situation you'd like to comprehend. Ask yourself what you think it is that matters to you. Answer the question, then ask why it is important to you.

Continue doing this at least five times , until you've identified and clarified the reasons you feel personally the particular circumstance is significant to you.

Journaling Prompt 3: Coping

This prompt will get you thinking about what you can do to reduce the triggers' power. Do you have a way to remind yourself the trigger is just an event and there's no reason for you to be so angry about it? If you are able to identify this point, you are able to begin to work on improving yourself. Find strategies that you can apply the next time you feel triggered, and develop a plan for yourself.

This prompt can be used as an opportunity to start to determine the way you react by creating plans. Keep in mind that the ability to establish a plan is usually more efficient than rushing into action blindly. That is crucial.

The Journaling Challenge 4: Write a letter to the child in your life

The final suggestion for dealing with triggers requires you to address the root cause of the trigger initially. There are triggers for everyone and most of them are created during the early years of childhood. It's time to address your triggers head-on. Send a letter to the younger you, in which you apologize for the experiences of childhood that you endured as a result of your triggersand stating that you are entitled to be secure and protected and that you are able to take care of yourself to recover.

This question will allow you realize that you're not responsible for your past behavior and you are not responsible to the conduct of other people. However, you can take action towards yourself and this can be done by taking the time to think about how you can change your behavior instead. It is possible that you weren't capable of protecting yourself in your youth however now as an adult you hold this power. Write yourself a letter to yourself to claim this power once and all.

## Chapter 9: The Journaling Technique To Discover Self-Development

Self-discovery is as the name suggests, all about discovering your self and what you're about as an individual. It requires you to get to know your self from the inside out and recognize the ideal that you have, who you'd like to be and how you can achieve it, as well as the other aspects of what you're. You're a complex mental being inside your mind If you aren't able to handle that entire complex individual, you're likely to have a tough experience navigating your way through life.

In terms of personal development, self-discovery is the primary thing you require. If you wish to be successful, be sure to discover yourself, who you really are as well as what you would like to achieve and much more. You must determine what you love and what your goal is. It is important to determine the person you'd like to be to achieve your goals. To discover your mission in life, you have to spend time and think about your life. It is essential to understand yourself as well as your goals and more.

We all want to believe that we know who we are in and out, however most of the time, it's not the case. We are missing out on a lot of important facts that we must recognize due to the way we make assumptions about ourselves. Fortunately, within this article, we're going to bring an end to this. We will discuss how you can begin to uncover your true self, and to be authentic to the person you truly are and what you can do in your write to achieve that.

What is Self-Discovery?

Self-discovery is the process of becoming acquainted with yourself. It's about discovering what you're like in your own way, getting to know you in person, and working to do all that can to ensure you are aware of what you're doing and the person you are as an individual. It's about understanding yourself better so that are able to work with your self in ways that enable you to become more efficient, more happy, and more successful than ever before, because you'll be aware of what you should do. It's all about soul-searching and discovering the ways you can improve as an individual. This will require you to recognize yourself, your strengths and dislikes, as well as other aspects. In reality, there are four major categories we will be examining in this section on self-discovery. However, you can be sure that there are other categories too. The four categories of self-discovery can be described as follows.

Discovering your passions

There is something that motivates you more than any other thing. It is likely to motivate you to keep engaged. It's something you can engage in for hours hours on end , but you never feel exhausted or bored as you are doing something you enjoy in the process. It is easy to lose yourself in your task--this is known as being in the flow state. Passion is the thing that you are able to keep doing for hours without feeling exhausted. It is very powerful.

If you are able to identify what you love to do and what you are passionate about, you can begin to consider what you have to offer the world. It is important to identify the things it is that you could do in order to live your life to the most authentic version of yourself, to discover your greatest qualities and goals. If you're looking to identify those things that you are passionate about, the most effective method is to make sure that you're making the effort to become the person you desire to be.

For some who write, it is their main passion. Others, their love is serving others through creating artwork, participating in sports and even cooking or something else similar. If you are able to identify your interests and you know what motivates your to become the most effective you you can be.

Finding your goal

Your mission is different from your passion. Your goal is discovering what it is that you're called to do. It's what you're looking to accomplish to impact the world. Thinking about the things you can do to make a difference in a world as vast as ours may seem overwhelming to some however the reality is that we all have an objective and are constantly altering the world around us. Change the world around you each when you assist others accomplish something, or smile as you pass them. It is possible to make a difference by doing things that may not been on your radar and could likely be your passion too.

Your goal is something you're motivated to accomplish. You believe that you must accomplish it in order helping others. It's there to be sure that you're working to make a difference in the world and you are happy when you do it.


Finding your motives

The next aspect you should think about is determining what motivates you to be. What are the motivations for becoming proactive that you want? What are you required to accomplish to be productive initially? There are a lot of methods to keep yourself motivated. Perhaps you have music that keeps you moving ahead, or you've got the practice of meditation to guide you to toward where you'd like to go or pray, or have some kind of routine you adhere to each time you need something. Whatever the motive is it's important and you must find it.

If you can find your passion in your life, you will realize that productivity is much easier to attain than you believed was impossible. If you are able to be motivated to do your best, you will realize that you are able to do better in the future. You can tackle the issue that you're currently in and start to work on overcoming it. It is essential to believe that you are able to be better and can prove that you are the person you would like to be.

Identifying your strengths and the weaknesses

We all are bound by our individual strengths and weaknesses whenever we attempt to accomplish something. It's just natural. We are only able to do what we can at any time if we're stuck. If you're looking to develop an attitude that is positive towards yourself, it is essential to be aware of which strengths you have and what weaknesses they are. Remember, there's nothing wrong with having weaknesses at all. In fact, all of us have weaknesses. The problem lies in not knowing your weaknesses. If you underestimate your capabilities or overestimate your capabilities, believing that you are able to do more or be better than you are than you actually are, all you'll do is creating difficulties. You are placing yourself in danger of failing due to the fact that you're trying to complete something you might not be competent to do. It is possible that you are working towards solving a problem or finishing the task that's too much for you even if it's not your intention to admit it. This will result in a lot of unnecessary cleaning by other people who are trying to clean up the mess you created.

You must be able to discern clearly what you can and should not do, not only for your own sake, but for the benefit of all who is around you. When you're able to do this and you are able to clearly discern the truth behind the situation, you'll be able to be more effective also. All you need to do is start to stay focused, remain motivated, and put in the effort. Journaling and meditation are great methods of assessing your skills and also.

Use Journaling to discover Your True Self

In the end, self-discovery happens when you're able to acknowledge and appreciate your authentic self. This happens when you realise that you know the person you are and what you were created to be. It occurs when you realize that being able acknowledge the person you are and what you're doing is the best choice you can do and in doing this, you will discover the person you are and know how you can stay connected with the person you are.

Journaling can help you contemplate your identity as well as what you're doing and why it's important. It allows you to determine what you are doing at any given point in time so that can start to improve yourself. It can help you identify what you are most interested in and what you need to do to become the most successful person you can be by allowing the desire, your goal and your drive to merge while making use of the strengths and weaknesses you have to begin with. Being able to uncover your own self while writing will allow you understand yourself more deeply. It can help you feel more calm and more connected to your self and more conscious of your potential of the things you would like to get out of the world.

Keep in mind that the entire purpose behind this journal is to gain knowledge about something new. The process of journaling is about identifying something about yourself that you didn't know or recognize before. It allows you to recognize ways to alter the way you react to yourself. It's seeing the person you've always wanted to be but didn't know about. It's a realization you can use the passion and desire and combine them to form something more than you. By completing these exercises you'll start to understand what you're good at and, as a result you'll be more content. You'll feel more relaxed.

The most effective method of journaling to gain insight into yourself really is contemplation. It's all about making the proper inquiries, and figuring out the appropriate prompts to aid you in pushing yourself ahead. You are trying to honor the most significant relationship that you have in your life: the one that you share with yourself. But, often, people forget about. It's learning to get over those convictions that could hinder you because you know you're in the right direction in the event that you do not acknowledge these beliefs. It's about becoming the person you always thought you would be.

If you're looking to begin to discover your own self, you'll discover the suggestions in this chapter very beneficial for you. This chapter will have you investigating your mind more deeply and more deeply than you've ever already done, looking for your interests and joy in life, so that you are certain that the life you live is one that you are content with the outcomes.

Journaling Prompt 1

As children, we all have things that we love. children that we adore unreservedly. We don't hesitate to express our love when we were small but as we get older as we get older, we begin to feel more self-conscious and immersed thinking about others and what they might think about us. Are you able to recall the things you were enthusiastic about as a kid? Was it something you were passionate about? Recall the time you were in your mind at six to eight years old. It's the time before you began to worry about what others thought of you. Take a moment to think about the things you loved more than anything else when you were an infant, regardless of how ridiculous it might sound. Consider that specific aspect and determine what you can do to make it happen. to incorporate it into your current life.

If you get focused on the opinions of everyone else it becomes difficult to be honest with yourself and, unfortunately as we age we start worrying more about others rather than ourselves. With some time it is possible to shift from this and begin to examine your own identity as a person prior to that moment. The point of this prompt is to help you begin reconnect to your passions and discover the things you loved earlier than anything else.

Journaling Prompt 2

Take a moment to think about your weakest point in life. Nobody wants to admit to having an issue, but eventually we must admit it at one point or another. Consider taking the time to reflect on the areas of your life that you are struggling with. Do not be afraid to admit it, even if the weakness is painful or hard for you, it's essential to admit it. It is important to acknowledge what you struggle with in order to begin to make improvements in the future.

This prompt should get you to start to think about your flaws within the global community. They'll try to hold your back, but you don't need to allow them to win over you. You can overcome them. You can develop yourself and work on your weaknesses in order strengthening them, especially when you're obsessed with them. Keep in mind that there is no requirement to be a master at everything, even when you are passionate about something you are struggling with.

Journaling Prompt 3

Take a moment to think about the things that you find beautiful about the world. Take a moment to think about the things you find extremely beautiful and moving. Do you think it's love between people? The dedication and perseverance that kids put into their attempt to become better? The unwavering commitment of the dog? Take a look at where you can observe beauty before you begin to consider the beauty. Note down what you think is attractive, and then consider the reason why it's appealing to you at first. After you've completed that, begin writing about how you can incorporate the idea into your life, and how you can apply it to yourself so that you can recognize how you're attempting to make yourself beautiful too.

This prompt is about bringing clarity to the things you are passionate about. It's about being able to identify what you are passionate about in this world and what you're willing be willing to accomplish to help bring beauty and clarity into your life yourself. It is crucial to be aware of this to be able to make plans for it. You'll want to demonstrate to yourself that you are genuinely interested and are determined to keep working towards the beauty you desire, and to staying motivated within your own life.

Journaling Prompt 4

Pause and think about your life to date. Consider all the highs and lows you've experienced. What is something that you're happy about? Why are you so thankful of it? What did it do to improve your life? What do you imagine you'd be today had this not occurred to you? What can you do to get this back later on?

This prompt is about acknowledging values and gratitude. This prompt is about focusing on those things around you that you consider to be extremely relevant and beneficial to your life. It is looking at two important aspects here to determine your own personal characteristics The first is that you are getting to understand what is important to you in your life. These are the things about you that are important to you. Did you have family members that you recorded? It's likely that you put a lot of weight on the importance of them in your life. And that's good! It's even good sometimes! However, you must be aware of what is driving you. This prompt also demonstrates the things you are grateful for and are grateful for. It helps you start to live a more positive life.

It helps you discover the positive side so that you can apply it to the future endeavors to progress. It allows you to hold on to something you can more effectively use for yourself and others. If you recognize what you are thankful for, you will be able to determine where you would like to concentrate your efforts in the same way.

## Chapter 10: Declarate Yourself Connect To Your Vision And Trust The Process

"It takes you half of your life to find out the person you truly are"

- Napoleon Hill

Khan was fascinated by the research and was interested in how he could use the formula and create his own brand during his peak times. He was convinced at the moment that there is much more that life is about than just being stuck within a profession which was not allowing him to fully realize his potential. He was confident that he was unable to alter his lifestyle in any way and begin with a fresh start and was seeking ways to strike an equilibrium that was right for his professional and personal goals, that was in line with his own personal values.

After a couple of days, Khan was able to meet Zara at the café that was next to the bookstore. After greeting him initially, Zara inquired if he was able to take time to go through the book.

Yes I did. It was an interesting thing to hear, Khan

Zara asked Khan about the areas Khan was interested in the most and what areas he was the most concerned about. Khan said that what he liked the most was the way a person can cultivate a passion to transform it into a world-class image, since Khan was always interested in the achievements of the young champions and child superstars . He wondered what formula was behind their enormous success. The answer was easy: they recognized their passion and nurtured it into an art form from a young age.

What do you think? Asked Khan.

Zara told me that the thing she was the most fascinated by her was the process of being made into overnight brand names and then fail utterly after an entire year or so after the hype has waned. Nowadays, with the advent of reality TV and social media the public is looking for quick success, and paying an enormous price when they reach the bottom. How often have we seen hip-hop artists, child stars or celebrities who are successful in the spotlight become victimized by their own success only to end by committing suicide, addiction, or even suicide? It's unfortunate because they have a long distance to go, and they could get over this obstacle by seeking help from someone who can help them or even a mentor.

Sure, that's the case. According to Khan I've always been baffled by why successful people with a promising prospects suddenly stop their lives. I've often wondered what the reason is? Whatever the reason, many think it is because they've been launched and are unable to handle the pressure of stardom or are unable to perform to their potential and which causes them to become lonely and lose their identity, to the point that they can't be accepted by society.

In reality Instead of being humble after their the success they allow their egos grow too big and become lost. It's sad to frequently hear stories of stars who are established and emerging talent with a bright future who abruptly crashing, Zara

Khan was still asking questions what the reasons behind why all these athletes or stars who reach stardom suffer no end in time?

Zara admitted that although they have enjoyed material success and fame, they've not been able to access a key element that is the P's "presence". She said that her father will always recognize presence as the most crucial element for lasting success.

In a moment of panic, Khan said could you clarify the "presence of the presence

Zara interrupted and said it's recommended to speak with the author of the book, stating that her parents had been visiting her on the weekend and for the duration of a month.

It's a wonderful thing to hear, Khan.

A day after, Khan was invited by Zara for lunch and to visit her parents. Though a little anxious and a little nervous, he walked to Zara's house and was welcomed by her father, who was referred to as Captain. They started talking and Khan admitted that he was enthralled with the model 7P featured in the book.

In appreciation of his words of appreciation, captain asked him if he had enjoyed the book.

Yes, I was completely captivated, and interested in the origins of the model 7P. Khan

The 7P Model is founded on my own personal experiences and my research into successful models from around the world across all industries. Everyone wants to be successful and successful, however the problem is that we're not equipped with the skills to reach the desired destination. Many people know of the reality that lives are a trip similar to a bus that is moving however, the majority of us aren't willing to jump into the journey and pay for the cost for the tickets.

Why? Asked Khan.

They are scared of moves and prefer to be an observer, even though in their hearts they would like to enter, but have conditioned themselves to believe that it's a dangerous route. In the world of life, there's nothing more exciting than stepping to the most dangerous places and getting the best out of you. Winners are aware of this and choose to get into their comfortable zone in order to win. They they are prepared to learn from and improve upon the failures. This is a huge difference in the game. In the world today, certain individuals live their whole lives without ever scratching the surface, whereas others have a smudge. You choose which route you'd like to go on, Captain.

"Most people know the fact that their lives are a voyage similar to a moving bus but the majority do not want to step in and pay for the price of the ticket"

Zara came on and spoke Khan's speech from the conference, which concluded with a teaser question asking"what is life? and how many have found ourselves?"

Khan Feeling overwhelmed, is asked to lead his thoughts on his life?

To me, the meaning of life is living with love, making a difference, and growing towards excellence. It is important to push yourself to become aware of yourself and transform into the most perfect version of yourself.

True, said Khan and asked why people aren't able to identify themselves.

They choose to follow the easy way and live life in a vacuum, without romantic or adventure. It is about learning every day through growing and developing one's fundamental identity. People have accepted the image that society has given them and don't know their authentic self. Another factor is that a majority of people seek quick, instant success, and are looking for ways to gain fame quickly through participating in reality or social media-related stunts and jumping into the spotlight. This is risky and it is recommended to follow the route that requires at least of three or five years prior to becoming stable, as Captain.

Are they really identical to the individuals who have been launched? And If so, what tips do you offer them? Asked Khan.

Keep your head down and humble and don't be a shill for the first three to five years, seek out an instructor, and continue the five-year process, said Captain.

Are these the reasons why the majority of talent that are launched fail and then disappear for good? Asked Khan.

Although there are many successful established brands that have been launched, there are numerous brands that fail to launch and don't last long after the initial fire has passed. The process of nurturing a talent that was launched is like replanting a mature tree and pushing to the forefront as a brand. Captain.

"What are the most important abilities that launched talent have to learn to last the distance? Asked Khan.

The discipline, the daily reinforcement, and stay in the background until confidence and confidence is built.

The Winning Pattern

The captain who changed the tone stated that the trip could open new avenues and help establish a winning formula for Khan's future.

What exactly is a winning patterns? It means that people know about winning patterns?

A winning pattern? Do you mean that people are aware of their winning track? said an enthralled Khan.

Captain, you are right. You have confirmed that the winners are aware of their patterns, and approach every situation in the pursuit of their ultimate goal, and accept the possibility of losing and winning as part in the game. When someone is aware of their own pattern of winning, after many years of self-reflection, understanding and study and re-convert this knowledge and strength into wisdom.

"But do people not become lazy when they're aware of the patterns that win?" asked Khan.

"That's an interesting question, the key to winning is not to be apathetic and teaches one to continue to progress until they reach a crucial moment in which uncertainty is overcome and one reaches certainty, as the Captain. He also said that successful people like Warren Buffet, Elon Musk, Muhammad Ali, Usain Bolt believed that they would be winners before they became millionaires or champions way ahead of others because they knew the rules of winning and believed in their process of building their identity every day.

The way they win is formed from their early days, through years of work determination, focus on trial and error, both winning and losing, until they get to a point at which you have a greater understanding of the road ahead. Every person is going to have a distinct pattern that is that is based on their efforts determination, persistence and determination to go the extra mile, despite being embarrassed or ridiculed. Knowing this pattern as early as you can will give someone an advantage when it comes to pursuing bigger goals.

"That's interesting. I'm interested in how one can gain an understanding of an effective pattern?

Young man, a winning pattern is created when one develops the ability to strengthen their bonds between mind and the subconscious. Many of us get caught up in the drama of life and have not established a healthy and positive relationship between them, and are being in autopilot mode. The bond between two people is similar to a lifetime friendship and the more one establishes a connection with one others and becomes more genuine, the more real they will be in their decisions, actions and making and staying at the forefront of their lives. The top leaders, champions, and winners are aware of their winning patterns through a close connection between their subconscious and conscious minds, and engaging in healthy conversations.

Are there any reasons why people choose to live safe and in mediocre ways, when inside they know they could achieve more? Asked Khan

The captain explained that the problem in the galleries is they've given up on themselves and made simple choices. When a person stops being a challenge to himself is when they cease living. The primary reason could stem due to a weak inner dialogue or the environment around them.

Captain, feeling elated Captain, spotting enthusiasm, said to Khan what your thoughts are on this?

To be honest I have also been in a long period of guilt being apathetic about reaching my maximum potential. The journey has allowed me to discover the true meaning of life and uncover my real identity. If I could ask what advice would you give to someone who is beginning over and re-engineering or creating the identity of their choice? I asked. Khan.

Captain smiled, and said "time is a precious commodity so take at least an hour focusing on your new identity , while working on your career to find an equilibrium level at which you are able to match each other. If you're still able to find the desire to go on, you'll discover the most suitable individuals and connections. This is the time that the outcome will be taken care of due to the power of nature.

We all play a role in this crazy world.

While the conversation was going on, they heard a loud echoe nearby and it sounded like an elderly lady in need of help. While at first it appeared like a private family conflict However, when they looked closer, they observed a sharp object lying that was in the hands of an intruder. They realized that the incident was actually a burglary taking place in the neighborhood. Despite the fact that there were a lot of people in the area and nobody stood up to defend the woman, fearing that the person in an hooded t-shirt might attack them. The Captain yelled out "robber the"robber" and then ran into the room He jumped up and took a golf club and walked downstairs into the area of incident. Khan was frozen, not knowing what the Captain was planning to do , and was then dragged as well.

Captain was straight at the intruder, and using a few martial arts skills, protected himself and knocked the intruder to the floor. He grabbed his neck, and was shocked to discover that there was a teenage underneath the Hood. Captain held the child tightly in one hand, and with a scary look informed him that he was given two options.

The first one is that he will follow in the right direction and the second is to have him sent to prison. After a short time the kid profusely apologised for his conduct and Captain demanded that he give the chain back to the woman he was able to rob. In a matter of minutes Captain told the kid to get out of the way before the police arrived and everyone was shocked. When the kid ran back, he turned and yelled at Captain, "I choose to go in the right direction, Sir."

Khan was able to feel this moment deeply in his soul and asked what made the decision to let you go?

He claimed that as the boy was held tight and gazed at his eyes, the noticed the terror in the boy's face, which indicated that he was lost in his life. His mind was instantly filled with images of his son who was born in Beirut.

When they returned and the Captain reverted to his normal self even as Zara's mom was yelling at him for putting her life at risk, the Captain remained calm. Khan admitted that it felt as if that he was in the dramatic scene, with a sense of humor and asked Zara whether her father was involved in martial arts. She confessed that her father used to play the role of hero, given the chance.

The Captain laughed in a loud voice and said "don't us all! We are actors all over the world trying to be heroes and if someone refuses this, they're lying."

He said that everyone is an actual drama but isn't able to accept it until the final scene is reached; the earlier people accept reality, and becomes more real, the better they will become. They stop living for other people to be a part of and instead focus on themselves and creating a positive impact externally. The world is shifting in the opposite direction , where the majority of people are focused on the external world , rather than their inside world.

What is the main motive behind this? Asked Khan

"Picture an animal spectacle," said Captain.

The majority of people who are actors are paid at a circus for a profit. They are continuously watched by their bosses, as well as those who enjoy their performances during their show.

Once the exercise is done and the animals are placed in their cages and forced to repeat the exercise on the following day and the day following After a few days, the animals learn to recognize that they are in the wrong and accept it as a fact.

A majority of people are unconsciously entangled to a corporate circus, and are consciously ignoring the situation because they've been in the same place for a long time. A majority of people are spending more than half of their time as part of the corporate circus, mostly being watched as paid performers and shifting from one position to the next, until they realise their situation and come to the point that they are exhausted or angry.

"This was the very first time I've saw the word "corporate circus'. When you talk about how each and every one of us is monitored, it brought up to me a frightening idea. What is the reason people are stuck and never emerge from the spectacle?" Asked Khan

The captain suggested that there are many possible reasons, including the fear of doubt, doubt, ego confidence, self-confidence or laziness but the main cause lies in "mental development" of the way that they have been taught from a young age.

In the circus, an elephant performs in front of the entire audience. watches, and then, when the spectacle is over, the elephant is ready for the next show After a few minutes the elephant realizes they've wasted their potential while being held in an arena. In the same way, many people do not realize they are in corporate circuses and feel no connection, and they lose their instinct to kill. The only reason one should stay in the circus is when it feels that one has contributed 10 times more than they are capable of and is creating a positive impact, thereby attaining the status of a superhero which is only achieved by engaging in a passion or a purposeful pursuit. In the same way, if you are stuck to the circus it's crucial to choose a passion or meaningful activity during the spare time that pushes one to be satiated with their own work.

"A person who is able to overcome the fear of uncertainty will be able to conquer itself and will not be scared to venture into the darkest of streets"

From where should a person begin, if trapped at the circus a time in the pursuit of their passion or reason for being or do they need to ask for more or quit the circus? Asked Khan

The main problem people face from the circus world is the fact that it's difficult to excel at something they hate, regardless of how hard they work. Disagreements with management can only cause further issues and personal concerns which is a sad situation that which is more frequently seen in the form of petitions and strikes from people who are struggling and encourage others to join their cause.

Let me go into more detail Let's say you walk through a construction site and see three construction workers making a wall for a foundation. When asked by each one of them what they were doing they all gave various answers:

* The second said, "I'm building a wall to make an income."

* The third said, "I'm working hard to create a wall and feed my entire family."

The third one said, "I'm building a beautiful monument."

Three of them do you think is the most successful? by the captain?

The third time, Khan

The third one has the highest success who is working towards a greater idea, even though it's in its early stages He also said that he will succeed in life, or help his children to become successful. This is the primary difference between earning cash or working hard, and one who has an end. The first two groups who work mostly for the sake of rewards and are not happy with their work and could be sufferers of discontent at work.

The other group is the majority of "gallery" that is predominantly middle-class income earners who are hoping for better things in life. They have found themselves in a situation they struggle to break free from, mostly because of fear or uncertainty. They bind themselves to careers or jobs that build the brands of others while not focusing on their own brand's identity. over time they lose energy and motivation to carry the extra baggage. They need to find the right setting and developing their personal brand and self-esteem, which can help them to grow.

Isn't the third party not establishing a brand for another? asked. Khan smiled knowingly. Technically it is true, however the most important distinction was the mental attitude that determines attitude. This, in turn, alters everything and creates an image for your professional or personal brand , said Captain.

"What tips would you offer to the other group of people," asked Khan?

It is important for them to learn to be smarter and not work as difficult, as if they don't they'll be replaced by machines and artificial intelligence. the issue with the two categories above is that they are not motivated in their lives and are dissatisfied in the process. Our purpose is what we live each day for and everyone should be aware of their goal before setting out to pursue their dreams or goals. And If they're not driven in their current endeavors then they should focus on any of the following fields to find their purpose or purpose on a full as well as a part-time basis.

They should be a part of:

* A cause

• A role of leadership

* A passion

The most successful people build their brand, not only during working hours, but instead at weekends or after work, by taking tiny steps on a daily basis, making it a routine. The gallery is a place to spend time watching TV and getting distracted with no reason A person who is creating a brand's identity is likely to spend at least one hour each day working on this as they build and expand their knowledge through reading, studying and modeling successful individuals.

What's your biggest regret? And if you're going to start again, what advice would give your self?" asked Khan.

It's true that every event has a purpose In retrospect If I could alter one thing I would have done it by spending time in the process of discovering myself and attain self-actualization. My advice is to pursue your passion as early as you can. Don't be concerned about the opinions of others and focus on the journey, not on the rewards, since the rewards will automatically arrive once you have a goal and adhere to the procedure. The journey of five years begins when you take one step now to build a brand that is world-class over the coming years. If you happen to meet someone who is successful or an company, don't ask how much money they have Instead, inquire what time it took them to establish themselves as a brand.

As the conversation grew more heated, Zara brought tea and some sweet treats.

Khan continued to ask what is the process of building an identity and at what stage does he determine whether he's in the right place or has built the right brand.

"That's an excellent idea," said Captain, saying that creating an identity is crucial aspect when you are you are pursuing your passion or goals, but most people don't realize that. I also had to go through a lot of years of experience and time before I settled on my identity.

Once a person realizes their true identity, they become real in their actions and the fear of being rejected is no further. They cease worrying about the unknown and embrace everything life offers them with a sense of respect, including the rejection and failure, said captain

The two gentlemen decided to end the discussion in the evening and come back in a couple of days to further explore.

The following couple of days Khan took time to think about his next strategy and think about the best way to proceed on his new path.

The discussion of the previous night made Khan feel more relaxed and Khan did not worry about his work at home, and instead began to take in each moment fully. Khan recalled the signboard at the cafe that read "successful people appreciate moments more rather than time". After a lot of thought after which he informed his supervisors of his plan to extend his stay by two weeks more. He while doing so, he realized that he was the one responsible for the breakdown from his marriage. He was able to let go of his excessive baggage and let go of his ego. In the night, Khan was able to make a surprise call to his ex-wife . They held a private father-son chat which was followed by a phone message at his family to say thank you to them for their kindness and love.

From that point on, Khan decided to enjoy the moment and began enjoying the small things that matter in life. He experimented with his cooking skills, trying Mexican, Arabic, and Puerto Rican dishes, enjoying the aroma and scent as he experimented with desserts. He went to the magic six flags mountain, and attempted the frightening rides that brought memories of childhood. He was relieved that the ride was enjoyable for every second of the time, not feeling guilty.

Khan was moved by the experience, and for the first time in his life his mind was at ease and ideas began to flow freely. One of the ideas worth mentioning was the idea of starting his own medical center for children with a particular attention to the most disadvantaged.

He was eager to share his thoughts his idea with Zara as well as her dad Captain the following evening.

"That's amazing Young man. Now you're taking your time and thinking strategically."

Captain also highlighted another important reason why many talents do not make it to the top even though they have found their passion or purpose but due to a inability to discipline themselves or not taking the enough time planning and implement their plan, they don't achieve success.

To mastery, one needs first manage oneself and master the art of making sure that one is consistent in achieving the goals one desires by making plans and prioritizing goals regardless of how difficult it might be.

If one knows where he would like to be, and knows the future holds so why wouldn't they make the effort to plan and sit down? Asked Khan.

Although it's not as difficult as it sounds the majority of people do not succeed at this point. This is because of a lack of discipline . They get distracted by their worries and forget their objectives. Planning is similar to cleaning up the storeroom. And even although it isn't easy to manage things but the advantages are overwhelmingly. In the field of speaking numerous qualified individuals who wish to be the best trainers, speakers, coaches, and trainers, aren't able to schedule time off to manage their paperwork and create material. The winner will always seek his goals, no matter what the result is because they are focused on the big image and are determined to succeed.

"Give the me six hours in which to cut down a tree, and I'll be spending the first four hours sharpening the blade" Abraham Lincoln Abraham Lincoln

In this life, in the end of the day, the ones who are successful are those who are willing to take a step away from their surroundings, focusing themselves to pursue their passions or align themselves with their goals and create an action plan to achieve this. The journey starts from the moment a person makes the first step in establishing their brand's image by taking part in the process, said captain.

The process was successful, Khan in general, what is the period needed to establish one's identity as a brand on the marketplace.

Captain replied instantly that I'd say the average is 3to 5 years from the moment one takes the first step and works on their daily profile and establishing the appropriate connections. Top brands like Facebook, Amazon, Airbnb, Alibaba, Apple or Skype might be considered to be well-established brands, but all of these brands has taken part in their own five-year journey and, somewhere along the way, they discovered an effective formula that has transformed them from a basic to an international brand.

It's awe inspiring indeed. I'm still a bit curious as to what took so long to answer Khan?

For those who found themselves in their early years might consider themselves lucky because they've been unconsciously involved in the process of self-discovery, and for others, it's an ongoing process of learning about yourself and unleashing the leader inside. If one can understand the psychology behind winning and has a desire to move toward mastery, they learn to take each day as an opportunity to building their identity on the five-year process. However, being successful in the wrong field is more risky than being average in the right field declared the captain.

"In real life, success in the wrong sector is more risky than being an average performer in the right field"

Many of the people who created their identity for the first time, like myself, experienced similar feelings when they first started out. But slowly, they discovered a connection to their mission or their passion, and then have shifted their direction successfully. The person who designs their branding identity may be the most difficult of the three categories since they're in the third stage of their career and might be a target for resistance. However , I believe that there's no ideal moment to reinvent yourself, and the earlier one steps on the game and plays the game, by taking part in the process of aligning with their goals or passions, the more quickly they'll discover the an identity. Be aware that the procedure is unique to every person, just like the DNA. Captain

What did you do to reinvent yourself and create a business model around this question asked Khan in a rousing manner?

It's different from my previous ventures , where I was a passionate beginning, I became dull towards the middle, and then burned out in the end in the process, I was hustling before settling on an agreement to either shut down the company or sell the business, I lost the motivation to keep going. However, in the educational side of the business I discovered a deeper connection because I was passionate about instructing and inspiring students to become entrepreneurs, leaders, and communicaters, and also developing a business focused on making connections with those who are right for them and using the latest technology. Each year, while hustling my job, I felt the inexhaustible enthusiasm in me increase and more focused on my goals and dreams. The company has been recognized as an effective business model that is based with a system.

A system? What kind of system?" asked Khan?

"Well the most successful people have created systems that they know about that require a minimum investment of 3 to 5 years into their systems that operate in autopilot. Making systems is the main goal of every Entrepreneur, and having an agenda will help the person more comfortable in the storm. Nowadays, I oversee numerous educational institutions, with more than one million students registered in various countries. My absence makes little difference in the day-to-day performance since we have developed an established system that has proven to work. It took me five years to create an effective system, and many more years to perfect this. The most successful people invest time and energy in building strategies rather than trying to quick way to make money and is often observed working with others who have been part of their own processes and built systems around. While the average person has one source of income the successful will have at minimum, 3-5 different methods for earning money. If you happen to meet someone who is successful Do not ask the amount of money they earn or what kind of car they drive, but ask them about the time they took to create their brand and establish an infrastructure."

## Chapter 11: An Unexpected Companion - When Conscience Meet Tranquillity

Khan was taking an extended vacation of two weeks and took the trip to Oxnard which is a cozy town which resembles a sophisticated Spanish city that lies on the southern coast of California to visit a close family friend. As he was enjoying his long vacation and a walk along the beach, he decided to go for to the beach. He was thinking about his life and contemplating what his future might hold for him. Even though it was exciting but also had feelings of anxiety as he looked ahead. He wasn't certain of what the next steps would go given that he'd already lived for half of his life, but found that there was a gap.

When he returned to home, he stopped off at an adjacent Starbucks where he ordered his most-loved mocha salted caramel. While sipping the mocha, his gaze was focused on the Barnes and Noble bookshop across the street. An idea popped into his head to stop by and pick up the latest book. He noticed people drinking coffee and checking their tablets on the outside, while others read inside the store. He picked a book from the upper shelf, titled "Think and get wealthy" which immediately attracted his attention. He perused some of the chapters and became fascinated by the contents. He picked the book up and walked towards the counter for checkout and saw an enticing line of people eager to make their payment. In that moment, the book was in his hands, he wondered if it was better to leave the book or wait in line until he was ready to pay. He walked around quickly and saw a large poster which said:

"Successful people live their lives in a moment, rather than in the course of time."

The realization that life's events happen in a moment and he was waiting in line and thought about how to live the moment. He then heard an old voice say "Hello Dr. Khan Welcome to Barnes and Noble!"

He was not able to communicate but he was able to welcome her at her door. It was Zara who was in her typical excitement and cheerful mood at the counter at the cashier's desk. She added she thought the novel was a fantastic option too.

"You have a job in this place?" asked the timid Khan who was taken by the surprise.

Yes, I work part-time on weekends. Khan said that he was seeking her out at the conference, and that she was delighted meet her once more. She replied with "It's that law!" to which he smiled.

Making the same mistake again He got up and encouraged her to take a break with him and have a cup of coffee. The woman paused for a second and then agreed, to his delight. They decided to meet later in the evening.

Khan was waiting eagerly for Zara's arrival. He sat in the coffee shop to read his book when he saw Zara walking toward the cafe. It was a moment of amazement at Khan and he felt a deep connection to Zara and it was beyond an acquaintance which was eager to be explored. Zara welcomed him with a comment she was pleased with his speech at the conference, and particularly the final moment, when he asked his crowd if they had found that life was indeed a journey.

We all are travelers through the wilds of this world. The best we will find on our travels is a genuine person to be a friend." - Robert Louis Stevenson

It was an unplanned question that came to me and I thought of putting it to the audience. Khan instantly changed the topic to her and asked her what is the meaning of life to her.

With no hesitation she said, "life is a voyage of discovery." Further, she inquired the motive behind the question, citing the message to take home.

Khan said"Well that's quite a lengthy story But if I go straight to the point It was a short but powerful moment that caught my attention. He told me the tale of the boy who was in the paddy field that brought me back to my childhood and forced me to think about the next steps.

Zara who was Lebanese and American, was in her late twenties when Khan was in his mid-thirties. As their relationship began to grow in their conversations. Khan saw a darker side that was hidden behind her bubbly personality. He inquired about how she managed two jobs. Her main job was event management that she shared with a colleague as well as her part-time job was a hobby project to keep her going by learning, reading and participating in book launch events. She also admitted that she is a freelance journalist. Her ultimate goal is to create her own event and publishing business.

"Creating the brand's identity should to be an ongoing job but it can be a part-time job that requires just one hour per day."

That's impressive! You're doing the American dream, and you've asked Khan openly

Yes I am, but my main goal is to further expand my vision within my home country and spread to the world. As the conversation got more intense, Zara inquired about the origins of the story of the boy who was in his paddy fields.

Khan slowly began to tell his story of the way he decided to pursue his career and was unsure in his mind if he'd selected the right career.

What do you think of your job? Zara

Sometimes I am happy and sometimes I am tempted to give up and heading to a place that is peaceful and away from the bustle and noise such as this long journey. He said "and this is the beauty of life , isn't it? You can't always have what you want. you must fight for your dreams and choose the path that is distinct between your talents and passions.

"So how can a person create a brand image?" "Do I have a name within the field of dermatology? !" asked Khan curiously.

Sure as you've worked in the industry for a long time and are recognized by the industry as an expert brand or without awareness. People are likely to call you Dr Khan since you've established your own brand image to the masses as lawyers, pilots scientist, soldier or CEO. What's most important is to ensure that the user loves their work, the activities they accomplish and feels challenged and grow each day beyond the financial rewards. It is only when one feels stretched and challenged to the limits does one acquire an attitude of growth and there is no shame in pushing yourself to the limits or feeling emotion when you gain from passion. If this kind of fulfillment is not possible to attain within one's profession It's essential to is involved in a hobby that you are enthusiastic about. This balance provides a perfect balance of satisfaction and survival!"

Wow! Actually, this was the very first time that I'm hearing someone talk about passion with such passion. Khan declaring that he's not certain if he realized this level of passion during his professional life, since he would often complain having to work hard every day, and that there were instances when he was not motivated.

He then asked if there are numerous success stories of passion, I've often thought why people don't pursue their passions? Where does an individual begin and how do you convert an interest into something worthwhile?

This is a great question, Zara and I also experienced similar feelings until I realized that passion is a process with four distinct phases that are can be applied to any person's life. The four pathways are:

* Nurtured: Individuals who were cared for by family members or a close friend between the ages 2 and 10

* Discovered: people who discovered their passions in the years between the ages 10-24

* Launched This is broad topic and the people who fall into this category cannot be defined in terms of an age range.

* Design-based: individuals who have developed their identity on the basis of their interests or passions between the ages of 25 and over.

Zara stated that the majority of people don't know about their passions. However, successful people follow their passions at an early age and transform into a profession If they're incapable of pursuing their passion they need to find how to incorporate it into their current job.

While amazed, Khan was a bit puzzled and asked whether it was essential to combine one's passion into the work environment or if it could be pursued on its own?

Yes, it's possible , as many successful individuals including business tycoons, presidents and professionals have full-time careers while engaging in other activities to stay active and others blend their passions into their work. When someone successfully integrates their passion into their career you will get an advantage in the determination to be the best.

Khan was recalling his desire in finding a link to his profession and after few minutes, a bulb moment sparked his thoughts as he thought of his passion for agriculture and the natural world. The idea of creating a natural organic medicines slipped by his mind. When he spoke about this idea to Zara and she listened, he was more energetic and energized with a total shift in body language , sharing details about the benefits of natural medicine over traditional medical practices. He also stated his desire to discover a cure the condition, focusing particularly on children.

What happens when a person sets off on a new adventure when they've already been to the halfway point of their journey? what advice would you offer those who ask Khan?

Life is all about choices. A person's choices today will determine their future or the day following. It is the most important ingredient of a great leader. If you are considering a new route beginning at the very beginning and then work on a smaller scale using your free time until one gains confidence in taking it to the next step and eventually, in the process, you will find an ideal place to connect your passion and professional experience to create a fulfilling journey.

"It's those choices which demonstrate the true nature of us much beyond our capabilities" -- J.K. Rowling

Khan felt awed and stated that he'd certainly keep in mind the conversation. He also asked Zara to tell him if she'd achieved the same thing in her professional life that was aligned to her interests.

Yes, I said. Zara My father insisted that we read at a young age. This developed into a habit. As the result, I take everywhere I go, to experience the joy of reading and to relax the mind. Actually, our home in Lebanon has a huge library that contains all kinds of books. It was the motivation behind joining Barnes and Noble where I feel at being at home in a world of books. My ultimate goal is to establish an publishing company that will assist young writers and authors across the world.

What do you think of the company that manages events? Asked Khan

It was created by a close friend and me as a pastime that turned into a business that is profitable while improving our profile, said Zara.

I'm amazed by your efforts and can see the link to all the choices you made linked to one another. How did you connect these pieces so well? Khan asked Khan in awe

Thank for your time! I'm sure in the past I also had to deal with a variety of industries , and often became frustrated after the initial spark had died and it was then when my dad introduced me to the 7P model that is a way of developing one's identity and exploring one's self. As of recently, I've been adhering to the 7P model and my lifestyle and work are in alignment with my primary values. I am able to find a link to all of the things I do and the choices I make.

What is this model called 7P Could you elaborate more about this?

The 7P model is a method which allows every person to create their identity on their values. The most significant issue for people is that they live only to get through the month but fail to consider the bigger picture that will ultimately determine their own life's story.

Khan was being overwhelmed for a while because it was quite some time since he'd been offered a dose of self-help to help his personality, which did not bother him at all.

Zara stated that she would provide him with a brochure when they next meet, describing the 7P model so that Khan will get an idea of the model. As the evening grew more cold, Khan politely asked if Zara is available to come back after which they decided to catch in the evening following and continue the discussion. When he returned home, Khan was enthralled by the insights of Zara and was seeking answers within himself and was eager to see her next evening.

Hi Zara, said Khan was watching her.

Khan stated that he was thinking about what she had said earlier in the night about creating a persona built on his passions and values. Khan also stated that his brain was searching for the depths with the hopes to see a glimpse of his passion.

It's an amazing feeling It's a wonderful sensation to discover your passion isn't it. What about you, did you manage to come up with any ideas for your interest? Asked Zara

The truth is, I was thinking of many things through my mind, and I wasn't certain of myself.

You must follow the urge.

What are your thoughts about you in this moment?

Uneasy, I'm not enjoying my work in the same way I'd like to", said Khan

I've experienced that feeling having lived through many years in my own confusion about who I was, currently I'm far from the person I was and won't get lost in my own identity.

What is the reason people don't adhere to their own identity in the first place, if it's so simple, questioned a puzzled Khan.

Strangely, many prefer the complex route instead of the straightforward one and become lost on the way. One reason is the perception or media of other people. Success to the majority is defined as the amount of money earned, whereas those who have discovered their own personal wealth is merely a byproduct.

"It takes on average five years to create an identity for your brand, as well as 10 years of time to turn the art that is a work of craftsmanship or design"

For them, success or creating an established brand is all about shrewdness, knowing what you want and staying loyal to their beliefs. The 7P model suggests that those who have pursued their passion for at least five years has reached a stage that they can be able to handle any circumstance and adapt to any scenario while building their brand in the market stated Zara.

Then she wrote down the 7P's in the bottom of the receipt. She then handed the receipt to Khan and stated that when one can integrate all 7P's then one will certainly be world class.

The 7P's are interpreted as:

* Passion

* The purpose

* Plan

* Process

* People

* Personality

* Presence

This is interesting, said Khan and further enquiring about what a person can do to determine whether he's following the right interest or calling, and how transform it into an established brand.

Zara told me that you will be able to feel in your gut that you're pursuing your passion and not a hobby that gives some satisfaction for a short time, but passion is more enduring and emotionally more enduring. A passion-driven pursuit will generate an unstoppable desire, and as each year passes, if your passion grows stronger, then it is on the right path. If you're in pursuit of something contrary to your core and you feel overwhelmed when the honeymoon phase is over. When you're on the right track in your pursuit, you'll see your energy flowing freely from the inside.

Zara added that creating branding isn't an option for everyone, however it is achievable for all. It takes lots of work and daily commitments until you are at the top of your chosen field. The key to remember is that anyone can build their own brand, regardless of backgrounds, gender or age. The sooner you realize it, the better, because developing it at a young stage will give them an enormous advantage over those who've accumulated too many responsibilities over the course of time.

Khan was interested to find out how one can build a brand for themselves and stand out from others?

In order to put his mind at ease, Zara gave him the small book that her father gave her upon her move in the US and stated that this was the first part of the three. She admitted that her father kept this book in a closed drawer for a long time, before sharing it with other people.

Khan asked whether the father of her was an politician, or some kind healing practitioner!

Zara was unable to stop her breath from laughter and said also, he's an educator and has spent a long time researching this model in the light of his personal experiences as well as studies of top-performing people who have succeeded.

They said goodbye that night as Khan returned to his home. He jumped right into the book he received.

## Chapter 12: Determine Your Purpose - Define Your "Why"

A sense of purpose is when one is in charge of the direction and actions and works on an ongoing plan every day to achieve a bigger vision. If we go to a different country , the first question commonly asked by an immigration official will be "what is the reason behind your trip?" Similarly, to be world-class, one needs to be driven to push them past despair and hardship to achieve the highest level of excellence.

What is your purpose in life?

Have you considered this issue? Consider for a moment the meaning of your life to you. What would you like to be perceived 10 years' time? What can you do to contribute to or make a difference that could have an impact on people's lives? What do you want your contribution to be remembered? These are the main elements that you should think about when you are determining your goal and aligning this with your goals and values. The more one is confident about the solution, the better their path ahead will be. The most common reason that people do not have motivation and direction in their lives is that they've been caught up in their jobs or careers without thinking about it, and consequently losing control over themselves. If a person is unmotivated it's similar being driving to an uninhabited place in pitch black with no lights on , and thus being lost, lost or confused.

"Why" is the underlying reason of your pursuit to perfection"

Imagine a person boarding the bus with a $1,000 bill, but they aren't sure what direction they'd like to take. When the bus conductor asks "where is your destination" this kind of passenger will declare that they aren't sure however, they have the money and is able to continue riding around. After an extended period, the passenger is tired and requests to get dropped at the stop next after which the bus driver requests for money and the person refuses, saying that he did not reach the desired destination or take pleasure in the journey. The conductor is confused and tells the person, "My dear, next time, first decide which direction you'd like to take before boarding your bus." This story illustrates many elements, the main one being that money alone does not ensure happiness if you're going towards the wrong way, and with no clear goals. The majority of people commit the same error when they enter the corporate world by boarding the wrong bus, not knowing the direction it is headed and ultimately getting lost.

From now on you must make a commitment to rise above mediocrity and be an inspiration in your field of specialization. In order to live your life its maximum, one must find the purpose of life by taking a conscious decision to step out of their familiar surroundings and pursuing your professional or personal goals. The main distinction between successful individuals and organisations, over the rest of the population, is the inexplicably clear vision. They make use of their vision as an invisible force that motivates their employees during times of despair and despair, thereby retaining energy or enthusiasm.

"Without vision even the sharpest passion can be a battery without the device." - Ken Auletta

Why vision is crucial

Vision is the intangible motive behind one's efforts towards the summit of Mount Everest. A lot of people who lack vision fail because of the inability to focus and social apprehensions that make them unable to stand up to the pressure. The winners remain focused on their goals during periods of uncertainty, they also accomplish smaller tasks with a never say no attitude. There are many instances where we hear of people becoming unsteady and rough in difficult times, in a state of anxiety, especially in the third or second phase of their career . They are spending huge sums in health and hospital issues , as they are emotionally unable to function. A person who has a goal is always up to the occasion and not allow temporary losses to cause them to fall. Legendary boxer Muhammad Ali faced several setbacks during his legendary career and with each setback came back stronger than ever before, due to his compelling vision. Ali's story has been an inspiration for millions of people to remain focused on the goals, regardless of the failures and setbacks that happen throughout the process. In reality, the more difficult the task, the greater the determination and the reward.

Q:) What distinguishes high-end brands from ordinary brands?

A:) A tree of success

Many organizations and universities are investing money in finding the difference that separates high performers and those who are average. The gallery features stars who are contemplating "what is that unique talent they have that we don't? The answer to this question lies in the goal they strive for and aligning themselves with their ideals. Highly successful individuals operate with an inner-out view and see the world as a shifting circular orbit. They are constantly reviewing changing, updating and improving their skills. Highly successful individuals have a long-lasting prosperity rather than just short-term glorification due to their mission and fundamental values. If carefully observed, many successful companies display their company's mission and vision statement in an area that is strategically to their employees and their clients, or placed in the company's chairman's or boardroom. If employees of an organization are committed and are working towards a common goal the contribution and culture of the organization are more important than seeking financial rewards or titles. So, every company should be able to communicate and get people to be aware of the values and vision of the company and strive towards an end goal that is shared with enthusiasm.

"The only thing more painful than being blind is to have vision, but not seeing" Helen Keller Helen Keller

Be aware of your purpose, passion and reward

The problem for many people of today is that they're unaware of their goals or have misinterpreted their goals by focusing on goals, passion, or reward, and then get lost in the process.

Here are some examples of incorrect visions:

* To be famous

* To be free

* To be immortally famous

* To be rich and successful

* To be able to purchase anything I can see from an open window, and whenever I'd like to

* To be famous and well-known

* To purchase an Ferrari or yacht

All of the answers are dependent on goals or rewards and do not have a motivation. The motivation is what propels an individual towards the goal. Here are some motives that can be outlined:

* Become the chief executive officer of a multi-national corporation

* To serve as the president of the nation or organization, or community

* To earn an Olympic medal

* To be recognized as an entrepreneurialist with a variety of businesses

* To be an eminent professional( lawyer, doctor architect, doctor etc.) and contribute to the community.

"Turn into a topactor, or no. one performer for the Hollywood or Bollywood industry

• To become the top inspirational speaker for the country, city,

The world or the region

* To set the pace in the field of technology.

* To become the world champion in your field of choice

"To be considered the most effective athlete in one's chosen field.

"To be considered the top artist, musician and beautician in the city, community or even the world.

* To become a manager of the country in an influential business

* Be the most successful parent to raise successful children.

* To be recognized as one of the richest 100 individuals in the United States.

* Top 10 most popular brands in the nation

* To be the number. 1 actress, model, TV personality, etc.

* To be acknowledged as an international filmmaker, speaker, author diplomat, etc.

* To encourage women to embark on their own entrepreneurial dreams

* To empower youth to become better leaders

* To give back to the community in the chosen field and to create a positive impact

Profit is the reward for fulfilling one's goals

Profit is the reward for achieving one's goals The winners begin the journey having this mindset with their eyes, which makes a an important difference when beginning out. When a person is certain of their goals then the next step is creating a plan of action for getting there. Someone who is primarily focused on the sake of earning money, without any clear goal may end up becoming wealthy but unfulfilled and could die in a sad way because they've never been able to enjoy the process.

What are you working on?

A story about a businessman who had was a full-time worker for a long time while keeping his savings in the bank up to the amount of $1.2 billion. He been spending most of his time at work and foreign missions , and much less spent with his beloved wife who loved dearly. In his numerous travels for business, he traveled for weeks and , at times, for months with no contact with loved ones at home. His wife was cared for along with drivers and maids who worked together for more than 20 years. When he was 47, the businessman was struck by an attack of the heart and died abruptly, leaving his estate in the hands of his wife. The story was that after a couple of years, the wife got married to with the chauffeur and lived with him for more than 10 years. Eventually, she also passed away, leaving the estate in the hands of the driver. In this moment, the driver was in a state of confusion and wondering whether he worked for the master, or if the master was in fact working for him throughout the entire time.

"Where there's not a vision, there's no chance of a future" George Washington George Washington

Have you figured out your goal?

The purpose of the object can be identified by following methods:

* An activity that is passionate and can be elevated to the top and then convert into profits

* A professional or leadership position that can be beneficial to the organization or across the entire

* To join a group or cause that can be beneficial and influential for others

\* Based on their desire to be loved by their spouse, children, or loved ones

Passion

Passion is the most effective method of identifying one's motives, whether based on profits or in a non-profit manner. A sensational feeling can be experienced when one is paid to do something they truly are passionate about and love. If someone is paid by doing something they truly are passionate about, an euphoric feeling emerges, which is not the case when doing work or an task where the energy decreases after a short time. If a person is involved in an activity they love can transmit that same enthusiasm at 3am in the morning, or at 3pm in the evening , with excitement.

Zenith Irfan's goal in life was to fulfill her father's dream of travelling through Pakistan and she set out to realize this dream. Zenith Irfan was a young woman who took a life-changing solo motorcycle trip across Pakistan In her own words, she described her triumph with powerful words : 'I felt liberated. Every person has an experience of their own that must be told to the world, by overcoming their own fears and accepting your new self.

Leadership

A leader's role in a bigger cause could be outside or within the organization, for example joining a group, club or community or even an entrepreneurial ventures that make an impact and challenging one's ability to lead. If there's no problem encountered, it's an activity for a short time and is not driven by a purpose. Leadership is a self-learning process, and it is best learned through experiences and challenging your comfort zone and taking on more obligation and responsibility. One of the first steps in discovering oneself is to enter the leadership role and to make decisions and make choices rather instead of merely watching and the demanding learning process of growing as leader is as precious as the gold spewed out by bubbling lava.

Robin Sharma was an established lawyer in Canada making an impressive sum. In his 30's Robin noticed a lack of connection and unfulfilling within his own life. On a trip to India He realized that life had a more profound meaning that was not confined to the definition of a title. He decided to work in forming the deeper meaning of life into a novel titled "The monk who has sold his Ferrari" that was an account of his own personal experience. As the days passed he realized that his life had more to offer than just the courtroom. He stepped into his next step of becoming an experienced speaker and author. The first seminar he held was attended by 23 people and 21 of them were his relatives. However, through perseverance and determination, he gathered the right kind of energy and carried in his new direction and is today among the top well-known leaders and authors around the world. His message is simple "lead without the name."

"A prisoner with a reason has more aspiration and hope than the average person with no goal who is locked in their mental prison"

Professional

This category is akin to entrepreneurs or SME establishments that contribute value to society. Many people start their careers from humble beginnings and attain a point of contributing to society and are living by this goal. They make their mark through solving a dilemma that they face in the market, by utilizing their earlier careers or by finding an answer to a problem they experienced to make an impact on society on a profits.

Nowadays, more and more people have their identity built on social media and their digital presence, creating a positive impact in their lives as well as other people's lives through providing value and service. Their business model is to find solutions to a new issue or bringing the creativity to an existing issue like Uber Airbnb Kapruka, Amazon kindle publishing, Udemy, Fiverr to list several.

Cause

A cause is as a time when an individual is involved in a cause or bigger than life projects that make an impact in the community's development. Famous leaders like Mahatma Gandhi Nelson Mandela, Mother Teresa, Martin Luther King, Rosa Park, Imran Khan, and many others worked tirelessly for the cause of a greater number. The cause doesn't have to be as massive, but can have a positive impact on people's lives by assisting the building of a hospital, school or even a well or helping victims in an issue that is related to your passion. Trail Sri Lanka, an initiative by two people that represent the private sector, which is dedicated to raising funds for the hospital for cancer by hiking from north to the south of the island. are projects inspired by causes. The Run For Their Lives (RFTL) is a different notable initiative that is driven by a particular cause.

The trauma's pain can be transformed into a positive effect

Sunitha Krishnan was raped by eight males around the age of 15 trauma she experienced was devastating and, after years of struggle and suffering, she became an activist to help other victims overcome the trauma. Today she has saved thousands of girls and has dedicated her life to this goal and has changed her appearance. A businessman M.S.H. Mohamed's life was transformed forever after he found out that his son Humaid was suffering from osteosarcoma which is a serious type that is a bone tumor. Mohamed was forced to undergo medical treatment through the National cancer institute (NCI) in Maharagama Sri Lanka and realized that cancer wasn't just life-threatening, but costly for treatment. In the hospital, they were required of an Positron Emission Tomography (PET) scanner. Many patients were suffering from the lack of the scanner.

## Conclusion

We're nearing the end of this book, as well as those prompts that you've been given. At your beginning you've been given 24 prompts that you can use to write in the event you aren't able to decide the best way to proceed. Journaling is only as effective as you allow it to be. The only power it has, the one that it is given when it's able to be utilized. You've spent the time to find out how beneficial journals can become. You've noticed how it can help in enhancing your self-image as you discover yourself in a variety of ways.

Journaling can be difficult to begin. It can be difficult to commit to, but the earlier you start journaling and the more productive you'll become. If you're looking to ensure that you're content with your life and feel like you're in control, you should be able to reach that goal on your own. It is important to monitor your own progress and improvement. You'll have to get to know you better and find out your motives to ensure you're sure you know the place you're at. As you concentrate at it, the more efficient you'll be and the faster you'll be capable of improving your own performance. As you work through these problems, you'll be more aware of. You can conquer the obstacles that were getting behind and start to gain a better understanding of your own self-awareness. That is the beginning of discovering yourself and understanding the way you interact with your own self as well as who you are as a person. This is that we should all strive for in our lives however it is an aim that isn't widely accepted by many.

It is important to realize that self-discovery is takes time. It's a process that is never accomplished. It's impossible to to fully understand yourself. There will always be something new or unexpected and that's okay. In the book we'll assist you achieve the entire thing. Learn to start writing down your thoughts to find out the person you truly are. You'll start to get to know your own self through setting goals and trying to achieve these goals. You'll learn more about your own self as you attempt to overcome challenges that are impossible to overcome in other ways. Learn to keep track of the progress you make towards your goal gradually and discover how to manage your emotions, and deal with any emotional triggers that you are fighting with your past. In addition, you'll be able identify who you truly are by following the guidelines that are offered in this guide.

From this point, all task is yours to take care of. You are responsible to stay on track on your journals. It's your responsibility to keep up with your writing, and to work to improve your own writing. At this point the book will only be beneficial if you are determined towards your goals and the sooner you realize this, the quicker you'll be able to start. Remember that you have the power to be a positive influence in the world. The crucial to your success in discovering within your hands. Are you ready to utilize it?

www.ingramcontent.com/pod-product-compliance
Lightning Source LLC
Chambersburg PA
CBHW050409120526
44590CB00015B/1887